jQuery UI

Eric Sarrion

Beijing • Cambridge • Farnham • Köln • Sebastopol • Tokyo

jQuery UI
by Eric Sarrion

Published by O'Reilly Media, Inc., 1005 Gravenstein Highway North, Sebastopol, CA 95472.

O'Reilly books may be purchased for educational, business, or sales promotional use. Online editions are also available for most titles (*http://my.safaribooksonline.com*). For more information, contact our corporate/institutional sales department: (800) 998-9938 or *corporate@oreilly.com*.

Editor: Simon St. Laurent
Production Editor: Rachel Steely
Copyeditor: Jasmine Perez
Proofreader: Jasmine Perez

Cover Designer: Karen Montgomery
Interior Designer: David Futato
Illustrator: Robert Romano

Revision History for the First Edition:
    2012-03-09   First release
See *http://oreilly.com/catalog/errata.csp?isbn=9781449316990* for release details.

ISBN: 978-1-449-31699-0

[LSI]

1331232962

Table of Contents

Preface

jQuery is a popular JavaScript library that is extensible using plug-ins. Some plug-ins, specifically those for managing the user interface, have been collected together in the *jQuery UI library*. These plug-ins help facilitate interaction with the user, and these interactions are simpler to manage if you use jQuery only.

This book covers the following extensions in jQuery UI version 1.8:

- Tab management
- Accordion menus
- Dialog boxes
- Buttons
- Progress bars
- Sliders
- Date pickers
- Autocompleters
- Drag-and-drop management
- Selection, resizing, and switching of elements
- New visual effects

Who Should Read This Book

All users of jQuery should read this book! More specifically, this book will interest people who want to improve the user interface of their websites and enrich them with new features.

Structure of the Book

Each of the features offered by jQuery UI (tabs, accordion menus, etc.) are treated in a separate chapter. Each chapter is independent of the others, allowing you to implement the functionality directly.

Conventions Used in This Book

The following typographical conventions are used in this book:

Italic

 Indicates new terms, URLs, email addresses, filenames, and file extensions.

`Constant width`

 Used for program listings, as well as within paragraphs to refer to program elements such as variable or function names, databases, data types, environment variables, statements, and keywords.

`Constant width bold`

 Shows commands or other text that should be typed literally by the user.

`Constant width italic`

 Shows text that should be replaced with user-supplied values or by values determined by context.

 This icon signifies a tip, suggestion, or general note.

 This icon indicates a warning or caution.

Using Code Examples

This book is here to help you get your job done. In general, you may use the code in this book in your programs and documentation. You do not need to contact us for permission unless you're reproducing a significant portion of the code. For example, writing a program that uses several chunks of code from this book does not require permission. Selling or distributing a CD-ROM of examples from O'Reilly books does require permission. Answering a question by citing this book and quoting example code does not require permission. Incorporating a significant amount of example code from this book into your product's documentation does require permission.

We appreciate, but do not require, attribution. An attribution usually includes the title, author, publisher, and ISBN. For example: "*jQuery UI* by Eric Sarrion (O'Reilly). Copyright 2012 Eric Sarrion, 978-1-449-31699-0."

If you feel your use of code examples falls outside fair use or the permission given above, feel free to contact us at *permissions@oreilly.com*.

Safari® Books Online

Safari Books Online (*www.safaribooksonline.com*) is an on-demand digital library that delivers expert content in both book and video form from the world's leading authors in technology and business. Technology professionals, software developers, web designers, and business and creative professionals use Safari Books Online as their primary resource for research, problem solving, learning, and certification training.

Safari Books Online offers a range of product mixes and pricing programs for organizations, government agencies, and individuals. Subscribers have access to thousands of books, training videos, and prepublication manuscripts in one fully searchable database from publishers like O'Reilly Media, Prentice Hall Professional, Addison-Wesley Professional, Microsoft Press, Sams, Que, Peachpit Press, Focal Press, Cisco Press, John Wiley & Sons, Syngress, Morgan Kaufmann, IBM Redbooks, Packt, Adobe Press, FT Press, Apress, Manning, New Riders, McGraw-Hill, Jones & Bartlett, Course Technology, and dozens more. For more information about Safari Books Online, please visit us online.

How to Contact Us

Please address comments and questions concerning this book to the publisher:

O'Reilly Media, Inc.
1005 Gravenstein Highway North
Sebastopol, CA 95472
800-998-9938 (in the United States or Canada)
707-829-0515 (international or local)
707-829-0104 (fax)

We have a web page for this book, where we list errata, examples, and any additional information. You can access this page at:

http://shop.oreilly.com/product/0636920023159.do

To comment or ask technical questions about this book, send email to:

bookquestions@oreilly.com

For more information about our books, courses, conferences, and news, see our website at *http://www.oreilly.com*.

Find us on Facebook: *http://facebook.com/oreilly*

Follow us on Twitter: *http://twitter.com/oreillymedia*

Watch us on YouTube: *http://www.youtube.com/oreillymedia*

Acknowledgments

Thank you to the O'Reilly team that allowed me to write this book (notably, Simon, Mike, and Amy), and to Daisaku Ikeda, who gave me the courage and perseverance to achieve this goal.

CHAPTER 1

Introduction to jQuery UI

jQuery UI is a set of plug-ins for jQuery that add new functionalities to the jQuery core library. In this chapter, we will install the jQuery UI library and briefly examine its content. The following chapters will detail each of the jQuery UI features.

jQuery UI Installation

You can download the library at *http://jqueryui.com*. Click the Stable link. This leads directly to a ZIP file containing the sources, examples, and documentation for jQuery UI. Once the file is downloaded, transfer the contents to a *jqueryui* directory.

This *jqueryui* directory now contains the following:

- A *css* subdirectory containing the CSS files associated with jQuery UI. You will see that jQuery UI handles CSS themes to give a custom look to the interface elements it manages. For example, the display of sliders may be different from one theme to another, as well as other items like calendars and tabs.

- A *js* subdirectory containing the JavaScript files for jQuery UI. This directory contains a compressed file of all jQuery UI features and the jQuery library file.

- A *development-bundle* subdirectory containing various subdirectories—*demos* (jQuery UI sample files), *docs* (files containing the jQuery UI documentation), *themes* (files for each of the CSS themes associated with jQuery UI), and *ui* (jQuery UI JavaScript files).

- An *index.html* file that allows you to view some of the features of jQuery UI in a browser.

Overview of jQuery UI

For an overview of jQuery UI, open the *index.html* file in a browser (Figure 1-1).

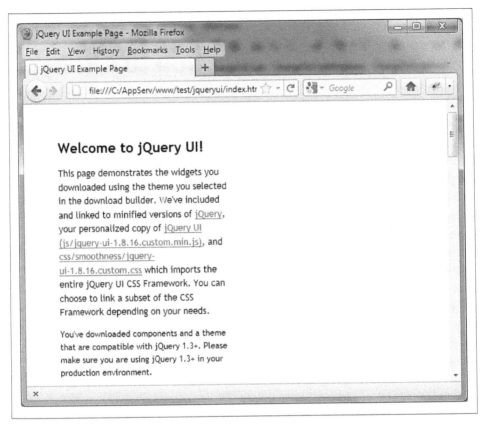

Figure 1-1. jQuery UI home page

In this file, you can see the different features that jQuery UI adds (Figure 1-2), including the following:

- Accordion menus
- Autocompletion mechanism for input fields
- Buttons and checkboxes of the nicest aspects
- A tabs mechanism to facilitate the display in the page
- Dialog boxes that are superimposed on top of the page
- Custom icons
- Sliders
- Calendars
- Progress bars

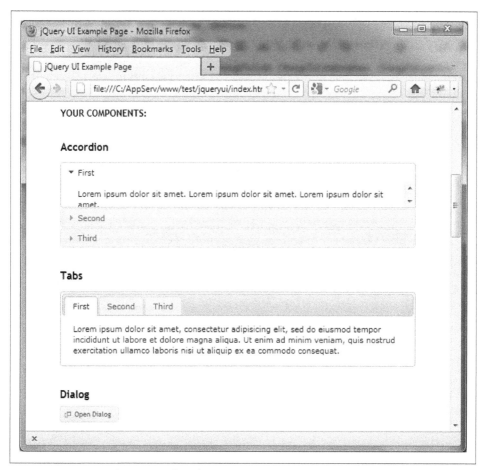

Figure 1-2. jQuery UI home page: list of components

These are all possibilities that we will discuss later in the book. We will also consider other mechanisms such as drag-and-drop, new visual effects, CSS theme files, and more.

What Is a CSS Theme?

What are the CSS themes we talked about earlier? To find out, just download a new customized version of jQuery UI, depending on the chosen theme. For that, go to *http: //jqueryui.com/download*, which displays the page shown in Figure 1-3.

Choose the UI lightness theme from the list on the right, then retrieve the ZIP file for jQuery UI associated with this theme by clicking the Download button. This ZIP file contains the same directory, but the CSS files included in *css* directory are adapted to the new theme. To see the look of this theme, view the new *index.html* file included in the *queryui* directory (this file will have overwritten the previous one). An example of a theme is shown in Figure 1-4.

Each theme provides a unique combination of background colors, fonts, and other screen elements. If we look at the *css* directory, we see two subdirectories containing each of the themes that we have downloaded:

- smoothness is the default theme downloaded with jQuery UI
- ui-lightness is the theme we just downloaded from the *http://jqueryui.com/down load* page.

Figure 1-3. Download of the jQuery UI with theme customization

Which Files Should We Include in Our HTML Pages?

In the previous sections, we have seen that jQuery UI is made up of different CSS and JavaScript files. In addition, some files are compressed, while others are not. Hence the question: which files should we include in our HTML pages to make use of jQuery UI?

Uncompressed Files

Uncompressed files are located in the *development-bundle* directory, under the jQuery UI installation directory (*jqueryui*).

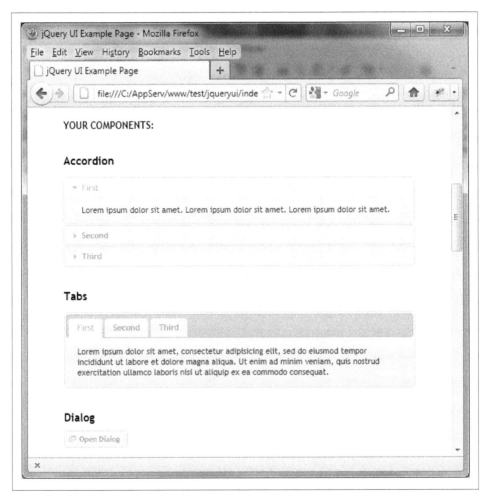

Figure 1-4. The ui-lightness theme

JavaScript files

The *ui* directory (located under *development-bundle*) contains the JavaScript files. The *jquery.ui.core.js* file includes the basic features (mandatory), while other files will be included only if required. The file ending in *custom.js* (e.g., *jquery-ui-1.8.16.custom.js*) brings together all the JavaScript files and eliminates the need to include each separately. The *minified* directory (located under *ui*) contains the same files in compressed format.

CSS files

The *themes* directory (located under *development-bundle*) contains the CSS files. It consists of various directories, each containing themes (e.g., the *base*, *smoothness*, and *ui-lightness* directories). Each theme includes an *images* directory and other CSS files.

The *jquery.ui.core.css* file contains basic functionality (required), while other files will be included only if they are required. The *jquery.ui.theme.css* file contains the definition of the theme itself (required).

The *jquery.ui.base.css* file includes all of the files in the *development-bundle* directory except *jquery.ui.theme.css*. The *jquery.ui.all.css* file includes all files (that is to say, *jquery.ui.base.css* and *jquery.ui.theme.css*).

Finally, the file ending with *custom.css* (e.g., *jquery-ui-1.8.16.custom.css*) includes all CSS files and eliminates the need to include each separately (it is identical to *jquery.ui.all.css*, except that it includes other files via CSS directives, while *custom.css* physically includes every line of all files).

Sample HTML page including uncompressed files

Here we want to display a simple page with two tabs. The main JavaScript file will be *jquery.ui.tabs.js* and the main CSS file will be *jquery.ui.tabs.css*. The main page will include the following base files:

```
<script src = "jquery.js"></script>
<script src = "jqueryui/development-bundle/ui/jquery.ui.core.js"></script>
<script src = "jqueryui/development-bundle/ui/jquery.ui.widget.js"></script>
<script src = "jqueryui/development-bundle/ui/jquery.ui.tabs.js"></script>

<link rel=stylesheet type=text/css
      href=jqueryui/development-bundle/themes/smoothness/jquery.ui.core.css />
<link rel=stylesheet type=text/css
      href=jqueryui/development-bundle/themes/smoothness/jquery.ui.theme.css />
<link rel=stylesheet type=text/css
      href=jqueryui/development-bundle/themes/smoothness/jquery.ui.tabs.css />
```

The *jquery.js* file is here at the same level as the *jqueryui* directory. This file is the standard jQuery JavaScript file.

The *core.js* file is mandatory, while the *tabs.js* file requires the inclusion of *widget.js* (as indicated in the *tabs.js* file).

The *core.css* file is mandatory, as is the *theme.css* file. The *tabs.css* file contains specific tabs definitions.

Now that we have the basic building blocks for the page, let's create and label two tabs and place some text in each. The following code goes directly below the previous code that calls the base files.

```
<div id=tabs>
  <ul>
    <li><a href=#tab1>Tab 1</a></li>
```

```
    <li><a href=#tab2>Tab 2</a></li>
  </ul>
  <div id=tab1>Contents of first tab</div>
  <div id=tab2>Contents of the second tab</div>
</div>

<script>

$("#tabs").tabs();

</script>
```

The result of this script (an HTML page with two tabs) is shown in Figure 1-5.

Figure 1-5. Our first program using jQuery UI

Compressed Files

The use of compressed files reduces the load time of HTML pages.

JavaScript files

The *js* directory (located under the jQuery UI installation directory, here *jqueryui*) contains the JavaScript files. Only the *jquery-ui-1.8.16.custom.min.js* file is needed here. The other file in the directory is the compressed version of jQuery.

CSS files

The *css* directory (located under the jQuery UI installation directory, here *jqueryui*) contains a subdirectory for each CSS theme installed (e.g., the *smoothness* and *ui-light-ness* directories).

Each theme includes an *images* directory and a CSS file to be included in the HTML page. This is the same file ending with *custom.css* (e.g., *jquery-ui-1.8.16.custom.css*) as in the compressed version.

Sample HTML page including compressed files

Here, we want to display a simple page with two tabs (as before):

```
<script src = jquery.js></script>
<script src = jqueryui/js/jquery-ui-1.8.16.custom.min.js></script>

<link rel=stylesheet type=text/css
      href=jqueryui/css/smoothness/jquery-ui-1.8.16.custom.css />
```

Only two files are now required in addition to the *jquery.js* file:

- The jQuery UI JavaScript global file (*jquery-ui-1.8.16.custom.min.js*)
- The overall CSS jQuery UI file associated to the style used (*smoothness/jquery-ui-1.8.16.custom.css*, associated with smoothness theme)

Now add the same HTML code that we used earlier to create, label, and populate the tabs:

```
<div id=tabs>
  <ul>
    <li><a href=#tab1>Tab 1</a></li>
    <li><a href=#tab2>Tab 2</a></li>
  </ul>
  <div id=tab1>Contents of first tab</div>
  <div id=tab2>Contents of the second tab</div>
</div>

<script>

$("#tabs").tabs();

</script>
```

The result is the same as before.

Change the CSS Theme

The great thing about CSS themes is that they allow you change the look of your page easily—just change the directory name to that of the theme you want to use. For example, let's replace *smoothness* with *ui-lightness*.

For each base file in the uncompressed version of the page, simply replace the smoothness directory with ui-lightness (shown in bold here):

```
<link rel=stylesheet type=text/css
      href=jqueryui/development-bundle/themes/ui-lightness/jquery.ui.core.css />
<link rel=stylesheet type=text/css
      href=jqueryui/development-bundle/themes/ui-lightness/jquery.ui.theme.css />
```

```
<link rel=stylesheet type=text/css
     href=jqueryui/development-bundle/themes/ui-lightness/jquery.ui.tabs.css />
```

For the base file in the compressed version of the page, replace the smoothness directory with ui-lightness (shown in bold here):

```
<link rel=stylesheet type=text/css
     href=jqueryui/css/ui-lightness/jquery-ui-1.8.16.custom.css />
```

The HTML page will now use the new theme (shown in Figure 1-6).

Figure 1-6. Our HTML page using the ui-lightness theme

And Now?

After this quick tour of what jQuery UI can do for our HTML pages, we'll look in more detail at each of the components, beginning with tabs.

CHAPTER 2

Tabs

HTML pages with tabs have become common in current websites. Tabs allow you to group a site's information by topic—this allows users to find relevant information quickly and easily by selecting the relevant tab.

Basic Principles of Tabs

Suppose we want to write the HTML code to display the tabs shown in Figure 2-1. We have a tab bar (containing three tabs here) and different content for each tab.

Figure 2-1. Tabs in an HTML page

To create this type of page using jQuery UI, we need the following:

- A global <div> block enclosing the whole
- A <ul> element to form the tab bar
- A <li> element for each tab
- A <div> element for each window inside tabs

Here is the code to create the page shown in Figure 2-1:

```
<script src = jquery.js></script>
<script src = jqueryui/js/jquery-ui-1.8.16.custom.min.js></script>

<link rel=stylesheet type=text/css
      href=jqueryui/css/smoothness/jquery-ui-1.8.16.custom.css />

<div id=tabs>
  <ul>
    <li><a href=#tab1>Tab 1</a></li>
    <li><a href=#tab2>Tab 2</a></li>
    <li><a href=#tab3>Tab 3</a></li>
  </ul>
  <div id=tab1>Contents of first tab</div>
  <div id=tab2>Contents of the second tab</div>
  <div id=tab3>Contents of the third tab</div>
</div>

<script>

</script>
```

If you open this page in a browser (Figure 2-2), you'll see that it does not appear quite as planned. For the results we want, we have to specify that we're using the jQuery UI tabs () method.

Add the following line (shown in bold) in the <script> of the page to call the jQuery UI tabs method for managing an HTML element with tabs:

```
<script>

$("#tabs").tabs ();

</script>
```

The page will appear with tabs.

The tabs () method is one of several jQuery UI methods used on a jQuery class object, returned by the jQuery () function. The elements of the associated list (indicated by the selector) are then transformed into tabs. When a user clicks a tab, jQuery UI will automatically and transparently manage the switch to that tab.

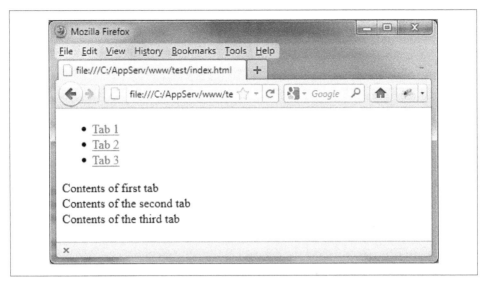

Figure 2-2. The tabs are not displayed in the HTML page as expected

Formatting Content

Using the `tabs ()` method drastically changes the appearance of HTML elements inside the page. Indeed, this method traverses (internally in jQuery UI) HTML code and adds new CSS classes to the elements concerned (here, the tabs) to give them the appropriate style.

Figure 2-3 shows the HTML generated by jQuery UI once the `tabs ()` instruction has changed the HTML DOM (Document Object Model) tree (the code was recovered using the Firebug extension in Firefox).

It is possible to use CSS classes of elements to customize the display. For example, if we modify the ui-state-default CSS class associated with `<li>` elements, we should get a new aspect for tabs. Similarly, if we modify the ui-tabs-panel CSS class associated with `<div>` elements, the contents of the tabs will change in appearance.

Modify these elements in the HTML by adding a `<style>` tag (shown in bold):

```
<script src = jquery.js></script>
<script src = jqueryui/js/jquery-ui-1.8.16.custom.min.js></script>

<link rel=stylesheet type=text/css
      href=jqueryui/css/smoothness/jquery-ui-1.8.16.custom.css />

<style type=text/css>
  li.ui-state-default {
    font-size : 10px;
  }
  div.ui-tabs-panel {
```

```
      font-size : 15px;
      font-family : georgia;
      font-style : italic;
   }
</style>

<div id=tabs>
  <ul>
    <li><a href=#tab1>Tab 1</a></li>
    <li><a href=#tab2>Tab 2</a></li>
    <li><a href=#tab3>Tab 3</a></li>
  </ul>
  <div id=tab1>Contents of first tab</div>
  <div id=tab2>Contents of the second tab</div>
  <div id=tab3>Contents of the third tab</div>
</div>

<script>

$("#tabs").tabs ();

</script>
```

The addition of our own styles must be done *after* those of jQuery UI, otherwise our changes will be ignored.

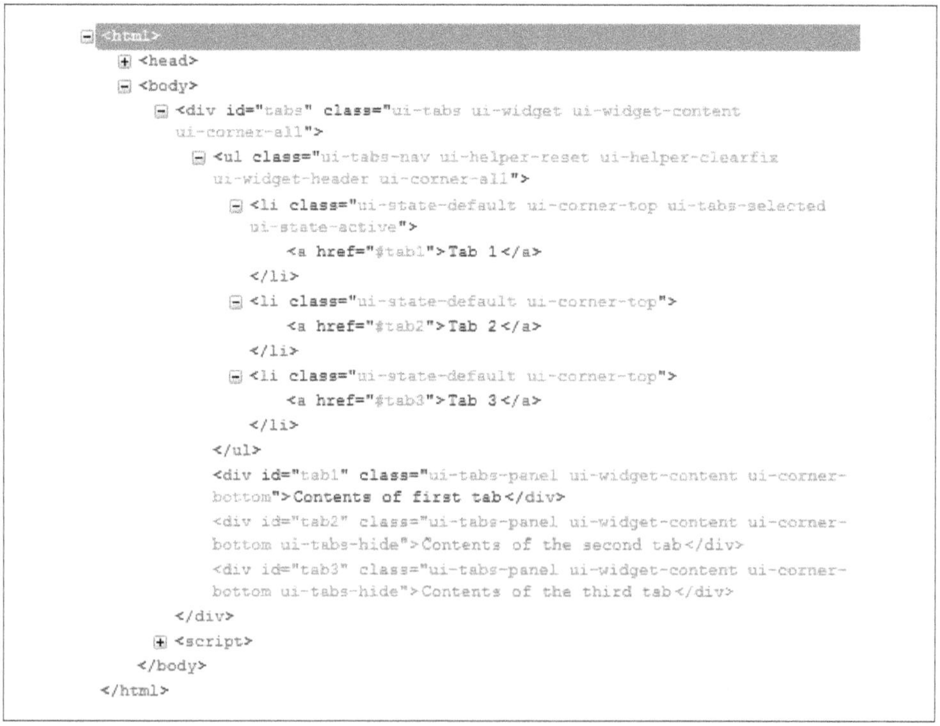

Figure 2-3. HTML code generated with the tabs () method

As shown in Figure 2-4, the appearance of tabs and their content has been changed according to the new style.

Figure 2-4. The tabs have been customized

The tabs () Method

The tabs () method can be used in two forms:

- $(selector, context).tabs (options)
- $(selector, context).tabs ("action", params)

The tabs (options) Method

The tabs (options) method declares that an HTML element (and its contents) should be managed as tabs. The options parameter is an object to specify the appearance and behavior relevant to the tabs. Different types of options are available, depending on whether they manage tabs directly or events related to tabs.

Tab appearance and behavior

Table 2-1 describes the options for modifying the appearance and behavior of tabs.

Table 2-1. Options for managing tab appearance and behavior

Options	Function
options.collapsible	Set to true, it allows tabs to be deselected. When set to false (the default), clicking on a selected tab does not deselect (it remains selected).
options.disabled	Uses an array to indicate index tabs that are disabled (and therefore cannot be selected). For example, use [0, 1] to disable the first two tabs.
options.selected	Indicates the index of the first selected tab. The default is 0, indicating the first tab on the page.
options.event	Name of the event that lets users select a new tab (the default is "click"). If, for example, this option is set to "mouseover", passing the mouse over a tab will select it.
options.fx	Indicates the effect that accompanies selection of the tab, such as a progressive display of the tab and its contents (indicated by options.fx = {opacity: "toggle"}).
options.ajaxOptions	Specifies options for Ajax (when you want to update the content of a tab with Ajax). For example, options.ajaxOptions.data allows you to specify parameters to the server.

Managing events associated with tabs

Some options are used for tab management, such as selecting, adding, and deleting tabs. These options (listed in Table 2-2) receive the **event** parameter corresponding to the event, followed by the **tab** object that describes the tab on which the event occurred. This **tab** object is composed of the following properties:

index
> The index of the tab on which the event occurred (0 indicates the first tab).

panel
> The <div> element corresponding to the contents of the tab.

Table 2-2. Options for managing tabs

Options	Function
options.select	The select (event, tab) method is called during the selection of a tab (either manually or by the tabs ("select") method call).
options.show	The show (event, tab) method is called when the contents of a tab become visible (manually, when displaying the first selected tab, or by calling a method like tabs ("select")).
options.add	The add (event, tab) method is called when adding a tab in the tab list (by the tabs ("add") method).
options.remove	The remove (event, tab) method is called when deleting a tab in the tab list (by the tabs ("remove") method).
options.enable	The enable (event, tab) method is called when activating a tab in the tab list (by the tabs ("enable") method).
options.disable	The disable (event, tab) method is called when disabling a tab in the tab list (by the tabs ("disable") method).
options.load	The load (event, tab) method is called when loading or viewing a tab in the list of tabs by Ajax (by the tabs ("load") method).

The tabs ("action", params) Method

Unlike the preceding `tabs (options)` method, this new form of the method modifies the behavior of tabs after their creation. The `tabs ("action", params)` method allows, through a JavaScript program, an action on the tabs, such as selecting, disabling, adding, or removing a tab. The action is specified as a string in the first argument (e.g., `"add"` to add a new tab), while the arguments that follow concern the parameters of this action (e.g., the index of the tab).

Calling these methods sometimes causes an event having the same name as the corresponding action (the `add` event is triggered by the `"add"` action). These events are processed by the options already discussed, and are listed in Table 2-3.

Table 2-3. The tabs ("action", params) method actions

Method	Function
`tabs ("add", "#id", title, index)`	Add a tab to the position indicated by `index` (from 0). Remaining tabs after the added tab will have their index numbers incremented by 1.
	`"#id"` is the id of a `<div>` element that is associated with the content of this tab (the `<div>` is created by jQuery UI, its content should be added later).
	The `title` parameter is the title of the tab.
	If the `index` parameter is not specified, the tab is added at the end of the list.
`tabs ("remove", index)`	Remove the specified tab and the associated content.
`tabs ("disable", index)`	Disable the specified tab.
`tabs ("enable", index)`	Make the specified tab active.
`tabs ("select", index)`	Select the specified tab—the content of that tab becomes visible.
`tabs ("url", index, url)`	Associate the contents of the tab with the URL specified in the `url` parameter. Ajax will retrieve the contents of the tab in the call to the `tabs ("load", index)` method.
`tabs ("load", index)`	Have Ajax retrieve the contents of the tab, using the URL indicated by `tabs ("url", index, url)`.
`tabs ("rotate", duration, repeat)`	Periodically select each tab according to a specified time `duration` (in milliseconds).
	If `repeat` is `true`, the cycle is repeated, otherwise it is done only once (the default).
`tabs ("destroy")`	Remove the tab management. Tabs again become simple HTML without CSS class or event management.
`tabs ("length")`	Return the number of tabs of the first element of the list for the selector used.

The bind () Method

In addition to event methods used in the options of the `tabs (options)` method, jQuery UI allows us to manage these events using the `bind ()` method. jQuery UI has created different events, listed in Table 2-4.

Table 2-4. jQuery UI events for managing tabs

Event	Function
tabsselect	A tab has been selected (manually or by the tabs ("select") method).
tabsshow	The contents of a tab became visible (manually, when displaying the first selected tab, or by calling a method like tabs ("select")).
tabsadd	A tab was added (by the tabs ("add") method).
tabsremove	A tab has been removed (by the tabs ("remove") method).
tabsenable	A tab has been activated (by the method tabs ("enable") tabs).
tabsdisable	A tab has been disabled (by the tabs ("disable") method).
tabsload	The contents of a tab have been loaded by Ajax (by the tabs ("load") method).

These events allow you to perform treatments using the `callback` method provided by the `bind (eventName, callback)`.

Examples of Using Tabs

In this section, we'll put what you've learned about tabs to work.

Dynamic Creation of Tabs

We want to create a tab (and its contents) dynamically using JavaScript. In the code shown here, HTML code initially creates three tabs, while the JavaScript adds the fourth:

```
<script src = jquery.js></script>
<script src = jqueryui/js/jquery-ui-1.8.16.custom.min.js></script>

<link rel=stylesheet type=text/css
      href=jqueryui/css/smoothness/jquery-ui-1.8.16.custom.css />

<div id=tabs>
  <ul>
    <li><a href=#tab1>Tab 1</a></li>
    <li><a href=#tab2>Tab 2</a></li>
    <li><a href=#tab3>Tab 3</a></li>
  </ul>
  <div id=tab1>Contents of first tab</div>
  <div id=tab2>Contents of the second tab</div>
  <div id=tab3>Contents of the third tab</div>
</div>

<script>

$("#tabs").tabs ({
  fx : { opacity : "toggle" },
}).tabs ("add", "#tab4", "Tab 4");
```

```
$("<i>Contents of the fourth tab</i>").appendTo ("#tab4");

</script>
```

Notice how we have chained the first `tabs` () method with the second. The first `tabs` () method is necessary because it transforms the HTML code we've written into a code that displays tabs (with CSS classes that jQuery UI automatically adds), while the second allows the "add" action, which adds the tab at the bottom of the list.

The tab is created by jQuery UI, as well as the `<div>` corresponding to its content. This content is empty, so we add the last `appendTo` () statement to add content.

The result is shown in Figure 2-5.

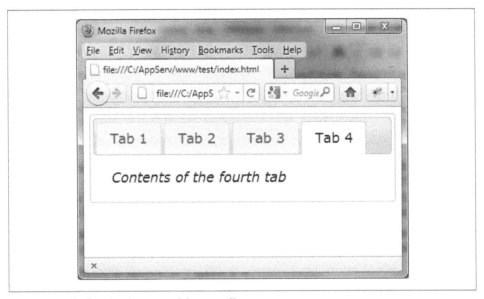

Figure 2-5. The fourth tab is created dynamically.

Modifying the Contents of a Tab Using Ajax

We now want to initialize the contents of a tab from the HTML returned by the server. We will use a PHP server.

We will modify the contents of the first tab, the index 0, using the "url" and "load" actions. The addition is shown in bold:

```
<script src = jquery.js></script>
<script src = jqueryui/js/jquery-ui-1.8.16.custom.min.js></script>

<link rel=stylesheet type=text/css
      href=jqueryui/css/smoothness/jquery-ui-1.8.16.custom.css />

<div id=tabs>
```

```
<ul>
  <li><a href=#tab1>Tab 1</a></li>
  <li><a href=#tab2>Tab 2</a></li>
  <li><a href=#tab3>Tab 3</a></li>
</ul>
<div id=tab1>Contents of first tab</div>
<div id=tab2>Contents of the second tab</div>
<div id=tab3>Contents of the third tab</div>
</div>

<script>

$("#tabs").tabs ({
  fx : { opacity : "toggle" },
}).tabs ("url", 0, "action.php").tabs ("load", 0);

</script>
```

First we specify the URL, then we specify that Ajax will load the content (in that order). The *action.php* file is as follows:

```
<?
  $txt = "<p> Tab content sent by the server </p>";
  $txt = utf8_encode($txt);
  echo ($txt);
?>
```

The result is shown in Figure 2-6.

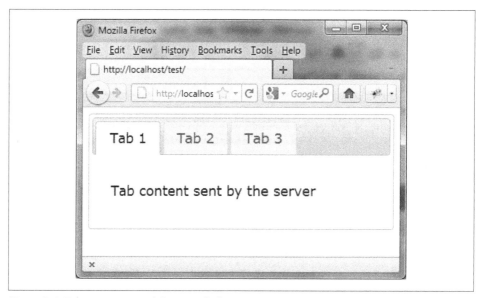

Figure 2-6. Tab content created dynamically by Ajax

Notice that, as we make an Ajax request in the HTML page, this HTML page should be displayed using HTTP (hence the URL in the address bar), and not by a simple drag-and-drop of the HTML file in the browser.

Next we'll take a look at how to transmit information to the server via Ajax.

Transmitting the Information to the Server via Ajax

This example shows how to transmit information to the server via Ajax to modify the content of the tab accordingly. In this example, we'll send the name and surname of a person and display it in the tab content returned by the server. The transmitted information (name and surname) is inserted into the ajaxOptions option in the data property (shown in bold):

```
<script src = jquery.js></script>
<script src = jqueryui/js/jquery-ui-1.8.16.custom.min.js></script>

<link rel=stylesheet type=text/css
      href=jqueryui/css/smoothness/jquery-ui-1.8.16.custom.css />

<div id=tabs>
  <ul>
    <li><a href=#tab1>Tab 1</a></li>
    <li><a href=#tab2>Tab 2</a></li>
    <li><a href=#tab3>Tab 3</a></li>
  </ul>
  <div id=tab1>Contents of first tab</div>
  <div id=tab2>Contents of the second tab</div>
  <div id=tab3>Contents of the third tab</div>
</div>

<script>

$("#tabs").tabs ({
  fx : { opacity : "toggle" },
  ajaxOptions : { data : { name : "Sarrion", surname : "Eric" } }
}).tabs ("url", 0, "action.php").tabs ("load", 0);

</script>
```

The *action.php* file, which receives the sent parameters and displays the contents of the tab, is as follows:

```
action.php file

<?
  $name = $_REQUEST["name"];
  $surname = $_REQUEST["surname"];
  $name = utf8_decode ($name);
  $surname = utf8_decode ($surname);

  $txt = "<p> Tab content sent by the server </p>";
  $txt .= "Name : " . $name . "<br />";
```

```
        $txt .= "Surname : " . $surname . "<br />";
        $txt = utf8_encode($txt);
        echo ($txt);
    ?>
```

The result is shown in Figure 2-7.

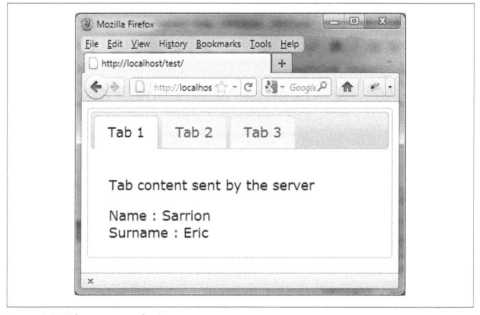

Figure 2-7. Tab content sent by Ajax

Using the Tabs add Method

We want to dynamically create a new tab, initialized dynamically by Ajax. The add event (triggered when inserting a new tab), can perform treatment, such as an Ajax call that inserts the content (shown in bold):

```
<script src = jquery.js></script>
<script src = jqueryui/js/jquery-ui-1.8.16.custom.min.js></script>

<link rel=stylesheet type=text/css
      href=jqueryui/css/smoothness/jquery-ui-1.8.16.custom.css />

<div id=tabs>
  <ul>
    <li><a href=#tab1>Tab 1</a></li>
    <li><a href=#tab2>Tab 2</a></li>
    <li><a href=#tab3>Tab 3</a></li>
  </ul>
  <div id=tab1>Contents of first tab</div>
  <div id=tab2>Contents of the second tab</div>
  <div id=tab3>Contents of the third tab</div>
```

```
</div>

<script>

$("#tabs").tabs ({
  fx : { opacity : "toggle" },
  add : function (event, tab)
  {
    $(tab.panel).load ("action.php");
  }
}).tabs ("add", "#tab4", "Tab 4");

</script>
```

The "add" action triggers the add event that updates the contents of the created tab:

```
<?
  $txt = "<p> Tab content sent by the server </p>";
  $txt = utf8_encode($txt);
  echo ($txt);
?>
```

The result is shown in Figure 2-8.

Figure 2-8. Using the add event

Using the tabsadd Event

Let's take the same example, but treat it this time with the events managed by bind (). In the case of adding a tab, the **tabsadd** event (shown in bold) is triggered by jQuery UI:

```
<script src = jquery.js></script>
<script src = jqueryui/js/jquery-ui-1.8.16.custom.min.js></script>

<link rel=stylesheet type=text/css
      href=jqueryui/css/smoothness/jquery-ui-1.8.16.custom.css />

<div id=tabs>
  <ul>
    <li><a href=#tab1>Tab 1</a></li>
    <li><a href=#tab2>Tab 2</a></li>
    <li><a href=#tab3>Tab 3</a></li>
  </ul>
  <div id=tab1>Contents of first tab</div>
  <div id=tab2>Contents of the second tab</div>
  <div id=tab3>Contents of the third tab</div>
</div>

<script>

$("#tabs").tabs ({
  fx : { opacity : "toggle" }
}).bind ("tabsadd",  function (event, tab)
{
  $(tab.panel).load ("action.php");
}).tabs ("add", "#tab4", "Tab 4");

</script>
```

We first create the tabs, then we intercept the **tabsadd** event. Finally, we insert a tab in the list. Be careful, this order is important, otherwise nothing works!

CHAPTER 3

Accordion Menus

Like tabs, accordion menus allow you to organize information on the HTML page. The information in blocks is displayed or hidden depending on the selected menu. The concept of accordion menus is that when a block is visible, the other blocks are hidden with an animation that looks like an accordion movement.

Basic Principles of Accordion Menus

Suppose we want to write the HTML code to display the accordion menus shown in Figure 3-1. We have three menu bars, each with different content.

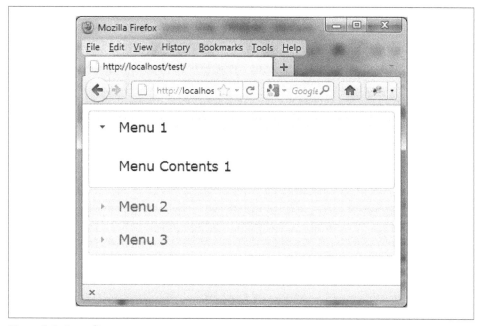

Figure 3-1. Accordion menus

jQuery UI requires us to write this as follows for each of the menus, one after the other (the title and content elements repeat one after the other):

- A global `<div>` block enclosing the whole.
- An element that will be the title of the menu: it can be a `<h1>`, `<h2>`, ..., `<h6>`, which will contain an `<a>` link that will indicate the menu text (and for which the href attribute is unnecessary, because it is not used).
- A `<div>` element corresponding to a content menu.

```
<!DOCTYPE html>
<script src = jquery.js></script>
<script src = jqueryui/js/jquery-ui-1.8.16.custom.min.js></script>

<link rel=stylesheet type=text/css
      href=jqueryui/css/smoothness/jquery-ui-1.8.16.custom.css />

<div id="accordion">
  <h1><a>Menu 1</a></h1>
  <div>Menu Contents 1</div>
  <h1><a>Menu 2</a></h1>
  <div>Menu Contents 2</div>
  <h1><a>Menu 3</a></h1>
  <div>Menu Contents 3</div>
</div>

<script>

</script>
```

When we display the page in a browser, once again, the result is not expected, but is a simple HTML page containing the titles and contents of the menus (Figure 3-2).

As we saw in Chapter 2, we must indicate in the HTML page that this display must be made according to the conventions of jQuery UI. To do this, simply indicate that the overall `<div>` is managed by the jQuery UI accordion () method. Add the following line in the <script> tag:

```
<script>

$("#accordion").accordion();

</script>
```

Notice the `<! DOCTYPE html>` header in the HTML. If this statement is not present, the management of menus is done poorly in Internet Explorer.

Figure 3-2. HTML preview of a simple accordion menu

Formatting Content

Using the accordion () method drastically changes the appearance of HTML elements in the rendered page. Indeed, this method scans the HTML and adds new CSS classes to the elements (here, the accordion menus) to give them the appropriate style.

Here, for example, the HTML code that appears after the accordion () instruction has been changed (Figure 3-3). This code was retrieved using the Firebug extension in Firefox.

It is also possible to use the CSS classes of elements to customize the display. For example, if we alter the ui-accordion-header CSS class associated with <h1> elements, we should get a new appearance for the menu titles. Similarly, if we change the ui-accordion-content CSS class associated with <div> elements, we get a new aspect for the content of menus.

```
<!DOCTYPE html>
<html>
  <head>
  <body>
    <div id="accordion" class="ui-accordion ui-widget ui-helper-reset
    ui-accordion-icons" role="tablist">
      <h1 class="ui-accordion-header ui-helper-reset ui-state-default
      ui-state-active
      ui-corner-top" role="tab" aria-expanded="true" aria-selected="tr
      ue" tabindex="0">
          <span class="ui-icon ui-icon-triangle-1-s"></span>
          <a tabindex="-1">Menu 1</a>
      </h1>
      <div class="ui-accordion-content ui-helper-reset ui-widget-
      content ui-corner-bottom ui-accordion-content-
      active" style="height: 22.8px;" role="tabpanel">Menu Contents
      1</div>
      <h1 class="ui-accordion-header ui-helper-reset ui-state-default
      ui-corner-all" role="tab" aria-expanded="false" aria-selected="f
      alse" tabindex="-1">
          <span class="ui-icon ui-icon-triangle-1-e"></span>
          <a tabindex="-1">Menu 2</a>
      </h1>
      <div class="ui-accordion-content ui-helper-reset ui-widget-
      content ui-corner-bottom" style="height: 22.8px; display:
      none;" role="tabpanel">Menu Contents 2</div>
      <h1 class="ui-accordion-header ui-helper-reset ui-state-default
      ui-corner-all" role="tab" aria-expanded="false" aria-selected="f
      alse" tabindex="-1">
          <span class="ui-icon ui-icon-triangle-1-e"></span>
          <a tabindex="-1">Menu 3</a>
      </h1>
      <div class="ui-accordion-content ui-helper-reset ui-widget-
      content ui-corner-bottom" style="height: 22.8px; display:
      none;" role="tabpanel">Menu Contents 3</div>
    </div>
    <script>
  </body>
</html>
```

Figure 3-3. HTML code generated by the accordion () method

Modify these elements in the HTML by adding a `<style>` tag (shown in bold):

```
<!DOCTYPE html>
<script src = jquery.js></script>
<script src = jqueryui/js/jquery-ui-1.8.16.custom.min.js></script>

<link rel=stylesheet type=text/css
      href=jqueryui/css/smoothness/jquery-ui-1.8.16.custom.css />

<style type=text/css>
  h1.ui-accordion-header {
    font-size : 10px;
  }
  div.ui-accordion-content {
    font-size : 15px;
    font-family : georgia;
```

```
      font-style : italic;
   }
</style>

<div id="accordion">
  <h1><a>Menu 1</a></h1>
  <div>Menu Contents 1</div>
  <h1><a>Menu 2</a></h1>
  <div>Menu Contents 2</div>
  <h1><a>Menu 3</a></h1>
  <div>Menu Contents 3</div>
</div>

<script>

$("#accordion").accordion();

</script>
```

This HTML code is identical to the previous, except that we added the `<style>` tag after the inclusion of jQuery UI styles. The addition of our own styles must be done *after* those of jQuery UI—if not, our changes will be ignored.

The menus and their contents now appear customized to the new style (Figure 3-4).

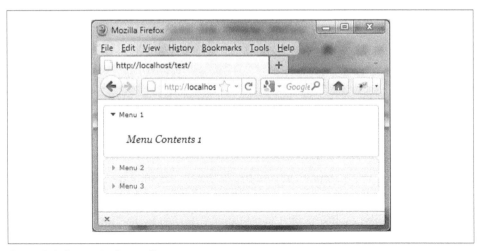

Figure 3-4. Customized accordion menus

The accordion () Method

This `accordion ()` method can be used in two forms:

- `$(selector, context).accordion (options)`
- `$(selector, context).accordion ("action", params)`

The accordion (options) Method

The `accordion (options)` method specifies that an HTML element (and its contents) should be managed as accordion menus. The `options` parameter is an object to specify the appearance and behavior of the involved menus. These options concern the behavior of menus, the height of content, or the events related to these menus.

Options for managing accordion menus

Table 3-1 describes the options for managing the behavior of accordion menus.

Table 3-1. Options for managing the behavior of menus

Option	Function
options.collapsible	When set to `true`, it allows users to close a menu by clicking on it.
	When set to `false` (the default), clicking an open menu does not close it.
options.active	Indicates the index of the menu that is open when the page is first accessed. The default is 0 (the first menu).
	To specify no open menu at startup, use `false`.
options.event	Name of the event that lets users select a new menu (the default is `"click"`). If, for example, you specify `"mouseover"`, users can select the menu by moving the mouse over it.
options.animated	Indicates a visual effect that accompanies selection of a menu. The default is `"slide"`.
	Other values can modify the `easing` parameter value in effect, that is to say, the way to progress in the effect (while retaining a slide-like effect).
	The possible values are: `"easeInQuad"`, `"easeInCubic"`, `"easeInQuart"`, `"easeInQuint"`, `"easeInSine"`, `"easeInExpo"`, `"easeInCirc"`, `"easeInElastic"`, `"easeInBack"`, and `"easeInBounce"`.
	Set to `false` to display the contents of the menu with no transition effect.

Managing the height of the menu contents

By default, menus will automatically adjust height to accommodate the height of the contents. You can also manually set the height. Table 3-2 lists the options for managing the height of menu contents.

Table 3-2. Options for managing the height of menus

Option	Function
options.autoHeight	When set to `true` (the default), the height of the tallest content is applied to all other menus. When set to `false`, the height of *each* menu corresponds to the actual height of its contents —the contents of the menus may therefore each have different heights.
options.fillSpace	When set to `true`, all the menus and content have the height and width of the global block parent `<div>`. The default is `false`.

Managing events related to menus

There are also methods for managing the selection of menu items. These methods receive the event parameter corresponding to the event, followed by the menus object, which describes the menus associated with the event (the one that opens and the one that closes). This menus object (described below) consists of the following properties:

oldHeader
> jQuery class object corresponding to the menu that is closing.

oldContent
> jQuery class object corresponding to the content menu that is closing.

newHeader
> jQuery class object corresponding to the menu that is opening.

newContent
> jQuery class object corresponding to the content menu that is opening.

Table 3-3 describes the options for managing menu events.

Table 3-3. Options for managing menu events

Option	Function
options.change	The change (event, menus) method is called when selecting a menu (either manually or by the accordion ("activate") method), after the animation has taken place (the selected menu was opened and the previously open menu was closed).
options.changestart	The changestart (event, menus) method is called when selecting a menu (either manually or by the accordion ("activate") method), before the animation has taken place (the menu that is due to open has not yet opened and the menu that should close has not yet closed).

The accordion ("action", params) Method

The accordion ("action", params) method allows an action on the menus, such as selecting or deselecting a menu. The action is specified as a string in the first argument (e.g., "activate" to select a new menu), followed by arguments that specify the parameters of the action (e.g., the index menu concerned). Table 3-4 lists the actions associated with this method:

Table 3-4. The accordion ("action", params) method actions

Method	Function
accordion ("activate", index)	Select the specified menu.
accordion ("disable")	Disable all menus. No click will be taken into account.
accordion ("enable")	Reactivate all menus. The clicks are again considered.
accordion ("destroy")	Remove menu management. Menus revert to simple HTML elements without CSS class or event management.

Event Management in Accordion Menus with bind ()

In addition to event methods used in the options of the accordion (options) method, jQuery UI allows us to manage these events using the bind () method. jQuery UI has created different events, listed in Table 3-5.

Table 3-5. jQuery UI events for managing accordion menus

Event	Function
accordionchange	Same meaning as options.change (see Table 3-3).
accordionchangestart	Same meaning as options.changestart (see Table 3-3).

These events allow you to perform treatments using the callback method provided by the bind (eventName, callback).

Examples of Using Accordion Menus

In this section, we'll incorporate the use of menus into a UI.

Opening Any Menu

When creating an accordion menu, the first menu (index 0) is open by default. Let's configure our page to open the second menu (index 1) instead. This is done using accordion ("activate"):

```
<!DOCTYPE html>
<script src = jquery.js></script>
<script src = jqueryui/js/jquery-ui-1.8.16.custom.min.js></script>

<link rel=stylesheet type=text/css
      href=jqueryui/css/smoothness/jquery-ui-1.8.16.custom.css />

<div id="accordion">
  <h1><a>Menu 1</a></h1>
  <div>Menu Contents 1</div>
  <h1><a>Menu 2</a></h1>
  <div>Menu Contents 2</div>
  <h1><a>Menu 3</a></h1>
  <div>Menu Contents 3</div>
</div>

<script>

$("#accordion").accordion ().accordion ("activate", 1);

</script>
```

The first accordion () method is required to create the accordion menu, while the second method activates the menu with index 1.

The second menu is open at the launch of the application, as shown in Figure 3-5.

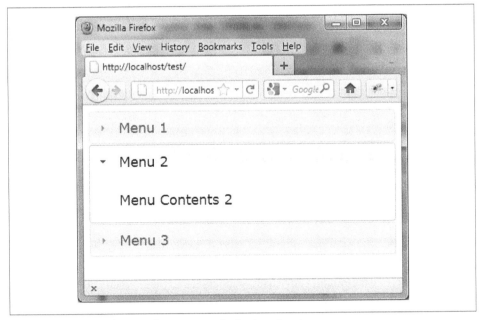

Figure 3-5. Opening the second menu using the "activate" action

Loading the Contents of a Menu with Ajax: Using options

Let's change the menu contents via Ajax when it opens. We will use the `options.change` and `options.changestart` methods. The `options.changestart` method will display a placeholder (in this case, "Loading") and the `options.change` method makes the Ajax call:

```
<!DOCTYPE html>
<script src = jquery.js></script>
<script src = jqueryui/js/jquery-ui-1.8.16.custom.min.js></script>

<link rel=stylesheet type=text/css
    href=jqueryui/css/smoothness/jquery-ui-1.8.16.custom.css />

<div id="accordion">
  <h1><a>Menu 1</a></h1>
  <div>Menu Contents 1</div>
  <h1><a>Menu 2</a></h1>
  <div>Menu Contents 2</div>
  <h1><a>Menu 3</a></h1>
  <div>Menu Contents 3</div>
</div>

<script>
```

```
$("#accordion").accordion({
  changestart : function (event, menus)
  {
    menus.newContent.html ("Loading");
  },
  change : function (event, menus)
  {
    menus.newContent.load ("action.php");
  }
});

</script>
```

The menus.newContent object is a jQuery class object that is associated with the menu that opens. The *action.php* file is as follows:

```
<?
  $txt = "<span> Response sent by the server </span>";
  $txt = utf8_encode($txt);
  echo ($txt);
```

To test this program, we must use a URL starting with http:// (e.g., *http://localhost*), otherwise the Ajax request generates an error.

At the opening of each menu, the "Loading" message appears, then disappears when the Ajax call is complete. It is then replaced with the code returned by the server (Figure 3-6).

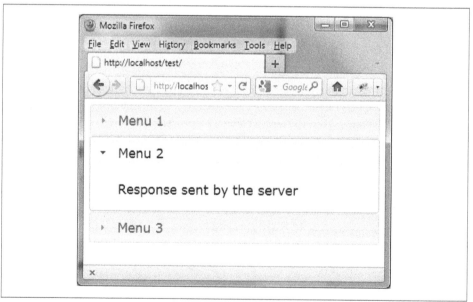

Figure 3-6. The code returned by the server via Ajax

We can also use the accordionchange and accordionchangestart events to initialize the contents of the menus. This is discussed in the following section.

Loading the contents of a menu with Ajax: Using accordionchange

This example is similar to the previous, but here we want to use the `accordionchange` and `accordionchangestart` events with the `bind ()` method. The code to do this is as follows:

```
<!DOCTYPE html>
<script src = jquery.js></script>
<script src = jqueryui/js/jquery-ui-1.8.16.custom.min.js></script>

<link rel=stylesheet type=text/css
      href=jqueryui/css/smoothness/jquery-ui-1.8.16.custom.css />

<div id="accordion">
  <h1><a>Menu 1</a></h1>
  <div>Menu Contents 1</div>
  <h1><a>Menu 2</a></h1>
  <div>Menu Contents 2</div>
  <h1><a>Menu 3</a></h1>
  <div>Menu Contents 3</div>
</div>

<script>

$("#accordion").accordion().bind ("accordionchangestart", function (event, menus)
{
  menus.newContent.html ("Loading");
}).bind ("accordionchange", function (event, menus)
{
    menus.newContent.load ("action.php");
});

</script>
```

The *action.php* file is as follows (this is identical to the contents of the file when we used `options.change` and `options.changestart`):

```
<?
  $txt = "<span> Response sent by the server </span>";
  $txt = utf8_encode($txt);
  echo ($txt);
```

CHAPTER 4

Dialog Boxes

Dialog boxes are interesting solutions for presenting information on an HTML page. You can use dialog boxes, for example, to pose a question to the user. HTML dialog boxes have the traditional behavior of other application dialog boxes—you can move, resize, and of course, close them.

Basic Principles of Dialog Boxes

Suppose we want to write the HTML code to display the dialog box shown in Figure 4-1.

Figure 4-1. An HTML dialog box

This dialog box includes text content and a title bar that contains a close button. Users can move the box on the page and resize it. jQuery UI requires us to use the following conventions:

- A global `<div>` block surrounds the whole with a title attribute that specifies the window title.
- The `<div>` content includes the content of the window.

```
<!DOCTYPE html>
<script src = jquery.js></script>
<script src = jqueryui/js/jquery-ui-1.8.16.custom.min.js></script>

<link rel=stylesheet type=text/css
      href=jqueryui/css/smoothness/jquery-ui-1.8.16.custom.css />

<div id="dialog" title="Window title">
  <p> Content of the dialog box </p>
</div>

<script>

$("#dialog").dialog();

</script>
```

The `dialog ()` method transforms the HTML code written on the page into HTML code to display a dialog box.

Notice the `<! DOCTYPE html>` header in HTML. If this statement is not present, window management is done poorly in Internet Explorer.

To display multiple dialog boxes simultaneously, as shown in Figure 4-2, we include the following (shown in bold):

```
<!DOCTYPE html>
<script src = jquery.js></script>
<script src = jqueryui/js/jquery-ui-1.8.16.custom.min.js></script>

<link rel=stylesheet type=text/css
      href=jqueryui/css/smoothness/jquery-ui-1.8.16.custom.css />

<div id="dialog1" title="Window title 1">
  <p> Content of the dialog box 1</p>
</div>

<div id="dialog2" title="Window title 2">
  <p> Content of the dialog box 2</p>
</div>

<script>

$("#dialog1, #dialog2").dialog();

</script>
```

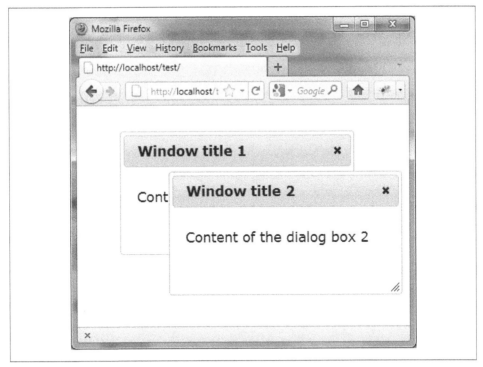

Figure 4-2. Dialog boxes displayed simultaneously

The dialog () method uses each element of the list corresponding to the selector (in this case, the two <div> elements) and displays the corresponding dialog boxes. They are stacked at first, and users can move and position them simply by clicking or dragging them.

Formatting Content

Using the dialog () method drastically changes the appearance of HTML elements on the rendered page. Indeed, this method scans the HTML and adds new CSS classes to the elements concerned (here, the dialog boxes) to give them the appropriate style.

Here, for example, the HTML code that appears after the dialog () instruction has been changed (Figure 4-3). This code was retrieved using the Firebug extension in Firefox.

These CSS classes can customize the display of elements. For example, if we change the ui-dialog-titlebar CSS class associated with <div> elements, we get a new aspect for the window title. Similarly, if we change the ui-dialog-content CSS class associated with <div> elements, we get a new appearance for the content of the windows.

```
<!DOCTYPE html>
<html>
  <head>
  <body>
      <script>
      <div class="ui-dialog ui-widget ui-widget-content ui-corner-all
         ui-draggable ui-resizable" style="display: block; z-index: 1001;
         outline: 0px none; position: absolute; height: auto; width: 300px;
         top: 0px; left:
         357px;" tabindex="-1" role="dialog" aria-labelledby="ui-dialog-
         title-dialog">
           <div class="ui-dialog-titlebar ui-widget-header ui-corner-all
             ui-helper-clearfix">
                 <span id="ui-dialog-title-dialog" class="ui-dialog-
                 title">Window title</span>
                 <a class="ui-dialog-titlebar-close
                 ui-corner-all" href="#" role="button">
                     <span class="ui-icon ui-icon-closethick">close</span>
                 </a>
             </div>
           <div id="dialog" class="ui-dialog-content ui-widget-
             content" style="width: auto; min-height: 0px; height:
             91.0333px;" scrolltop="0" scrollleft="0">
                 <p> Content of the dialog box</p>
             </div>
             <div class="ui-resizable-handle ui-resizable-n"></div>
             <div class="ui-resizable-handle ui-resizable-e"></div>
             <div class="ui-resizable-handle ui-resizable-s"></div>
             <div class="ui-resizable-handle ui-resizable-w"></div>
             <div class="ui-resizable-handle ui-resizable-se ui-icon ui-icon-
             gripsmall-diagonal-se ui-icon-grip-diagonal-se" style="z-index:
             1001;"></div>
             <div class="ui-resizable-handle ui-resizable-sw" style="z-index:
             1002;"></div>
             <div class="ui-resizable-handle ui-resizable-ne" style="z-index:
             1003;"></div>
             <div class="ui-resizable-handle ui-resizable-nw" style="z-index:
             1004;"></div>
         </div>
     </body>
 </html>
```

Figure 4-3. HTML code generated with the dialog () method

Modify these elements (shown in bold) in the HTML by adding a `<style>` tag to obtain
the layout shown in Figure 4-4:

```
<!DOCTYPE html>
<script src = jquery.js></script>
<script src = jqueryui/js/jquery-ui-1.8.16.custom.min.js></script>

<link rel=stylesheet type=text/css
      href=jqueryui/css/smoothness/jquery-ui-1.8.16.custom.css />

<style type=text/css>
  div.ui-dialog-titlebar {
    font-size : 10px;
  }
```

```
   div.ui-dialog-content {
     font-size : 15px;
     font-family : georgia;
     font-style : italic;
   }
</style>

<div id="dialog" title="Window title">
  <p> Content of the dialog box</p>
</div>

<script>

$("#dialog").dialog();

</script>
```

Figure 4-4. A customized dialog box

This HTML code is identical to the previous, except that we added the <style> tag after the inclusion of the jQuery UI styles. The addition of our own styles must be done after those of jQuery UI, otherwise our changes will be ignored.

The dialog () Method

The dialog () method can be used in two forms:

- $(selector, context).dialog (options)
- $(selector, context).dialog ("action", params)

The dialog (options) Method

The dialog (options) method declares that an HTML element (and its contents) should be administered in the form of a dialog box. The options parameter is an object that specifies the appearance and behavior of that window. The available options manage the appearance, position, and size of the window, as well as the behavior of visual effects.

Table 4-1 describes the option for managing the appearance of the dialog box.

Table 4-1. Options for managing dialog box appearance

Options	Function
options.title	Give a title to the window.
options.buttons	Add buttons in the dialog box. These are listed as objects, and each property is the text on the button. The value is a callback function called when the user clicks the button.

Table 4-2 describes the options for managing the position of the dialog box.

Table 4-2. Options for managing dialog box position in the page

Options	Function
options.position	The position of the window is specified as coordinates [left, top] or a string such as:

- "left top", "top right", "bottom left", or "right bottom" (for each of the four corners of the page)
- "top" or "bottom" (top or bottom, centered in width)
- "left" or "right" (left or right, centered in height)
- "center" (centered in width and height)

By default, the window is centered in the width and height ("center").

Table 4-3 describes the options for managing the size of the dialog box.

Table 4-3. Options for managing dialog box size

Options	Function
options.height	The initial height (in pixels) of the dialog box. The default value is "auto" (the size adjusts automatically to display all content).
options.width	The initial width (in pixels) of the dialog box. The default is 300.
options.maxHeight	Maximum height (in pixels) to which the dialog box can be resized.
options.maxWidth	Maximum width (in pixels) to which the dialog box can be resized.
options.minHeight	Minimum height (in pixels) to which the dialog box can be resized. The default value is 150.
options.minWidth	Minimum height (in pixels) to which the dialog box can be resized. The default value is 150.

Managing the visual effects on the dialog box

It is also possible, thanks to jQuery UI, to specify an effect for the appearance and disappearance of the dialog box with the options.show and options.hide options (described in Table 4-4).

Table 4-4. Options for managing visual effects

Options	Function
options.show	Visual effect to occur at the appearance of the dialog box (the effects are listed in Table 4-5). When set to false (the default), there is no visual effect associated with the appearance of the dialog box.
options.hide	Visual effect to occur at the disappearance of the dialog box (listed in the table below). When set to false (the default), there is no visual effect associated with the disappearance of the dialog box.

Table 4-5. Effects provided by jQuery UI

Effect name	Function
"blind"	The element appears or disappears from the top.
"bounce"	The element appears or disappears fitfully, in a vertical movement.
"clip"	The element appears or disappears vertically from the center.
"drop"	The element appears or disappears from the left, with a change of opacity.
"fold"	The element appears or disappears from the top left corner.
"highlight"	The element appears or disappears with variations of opacity and background color.
"puff"	The element is scaled from its center. It appears by "shrinking" and disappears by "growing."
"pulsate"	The element appears or disappears by flashing.
"scale"	The element is scaled from its center. It disappears by shrinking and appears by growing.
"slide"	The element appears or disappears from its right side.

Managing the behavior of the dialog box

Table 4-6 describes the options for managing the behavior of the dialog box when it is opened, moved, stacked, and resized.

Table 4-6. Options for managing dialog box behavior

Options	Function
options.autoOpen	If true (the default), the dialog box opens with the call to the dialog (options) method.
	If false, the dialog box is created, but will only be visible by calling the dialog ("open") method.
options.draggable	If true (the default), the dialog box can be moved on the page.
options.resizable	If true (the default), the dialog box can be resized on the page.
options.modal	If true, the dialog box is modal (other elements on the page outside the dialog box are inaccessible).
	The default value is false (the dialog box is not modal).
options.stack	If true (the default), the dialog box can be stacked (clicking on a window or dialog box brings it to the foreground).
	If false, dialog boxes are open, one on top of another, but users cannot change the order of the stack.

Managing events in the dialog box

Dialog box event methods (described in Table 4-7) allow you to perform treatments at different stages of the dialog box. They correspond to callback functions called at these different stages. The value in the callback function is the `<div>` element associated with the contents of the dialog box.

Table 4-7. Options for managing dialog box events

Options	Function
options.focus	The focus (event) method is called whenever the dialog box is activated (in its first appearance and each click on it).
options.open	The open (event) method is called whenever the window is displayed (in its first appearance or following calls to the dialog ("open") method).
options.beforeclose	The beforeclose (event) method is called whenever the dialog box will be closed (when clicking on the close button or making a call to the dialog ("close") method). If the function returns false, the dialog box will not be closed. A closed dialog box can be reopened by dialog ("open").
options.close	The close (event) method is called whenever the dialog box is closed (when clicking on the close button or call to the dialog ("close") method). A closed dialog box can be reopened by dialog ("open").
options.drag	The drag (event) method is called for every mouse movement when the dialog box is moved on the page.

Options	Function
options.dragStart	The dragStart (event) method is called at the beginning of the movement of the dialog box on the page.
options.dragStop	The dragStop (event) method is called at the end of movement of the dialog box on the page (when the mouse button is released).
options.resize	The resize (event) method called for every mouse movement when the dialog box is resized on the page.
options.resizeStart	The resizeStart (event) method is called at the beginning of resizing the dialog box on the page.
options.resizeStop	The resizeStop (event) method is called at the end of resizing the dialog box on the page (when the mouse button is released).

The dialog ("action", params) Method

The dialog ("action", params) method can perform an action on the dialog box, such as opening or closing it. The action is specified as a string in the first "action" argument (e.g., "open" to open a window).

Table 4-8 describes the actions you can perform using this method.

Table 4-8. The dialog ("action", params) method actions

Method	Function
dialog ("open")	Open the dialog box.
dialog ("close")	Close the dialog box. It is then hidden and may be reopened by dialog ("open").
dialog ("destroy")	Remove dialog box management. Dialog boxes are reverted to simple HTML without CSS class or event management, and are hidden in the page.
dialog ("disable")	Make the dialog box appear disabled, without actually disabling it. The dialog box elements (title bar, content, borders) remain available.
dialog ("enable")	Restore the normal appearance to the elements of the dialog box.
dialog ("isOpen")	Returns true if one of the dialog boxes in the list is open, otherwise returns false.
dialog ("moveToTop")	Position the corresponding dialog boxes to the foreground (on top of the others).
dialog ("option", param)	Get the value of the specified param option. This option corresponds to one of those used in the dialog (options) method.
dialog ("option", param, value)	Changes the value of the param option. This option corresponds to one of those used in the dialog (options) method.

Event Handling in Dialog Boxes with bind ()

In addition to event methods in the options of the dialog (options) method, it is possible to manage these events using the bind () method.

These events allow you to perform treatments using the `callback` method provided by the `bind` (`eventName`, `callback`). Table 4-9 describes the options for managing dialog boxes with `bind` ().

Table 4-9. jQuery UI events for managing dialog boxes with bind()

Event	Function
dialogfocus	Same meaning as `options.focus`.
dialogopen	Same meaning as `options.open`.
dialogbeforeclose	Same meaning as `options.beforeClose`.
dialogclose	Same meaning as `options.close`.
dialogdrag	Same meaning as `options.drag`.
dialogdragstart	Same meaning as `options.dragStart`.
dialogdragstop	Same meaning as `options.dragStop`.
dialogresize	Same meaning as `options.resize`.
dialogresizestart	Same meaning as `options.resizeStart`.
dialogresizestop	Same meaning as `options.resizeStop`.

Examples of Using Dialog Boxes

Let's put some dialog boxes in our script and manage them using the information in this chapter.

Opening and Closing a Dialog Box

Here, we'll use the `dialog` ("open") and `dialog` ("close") methods (shown in bold) to add two Open and Close buttons to the page for opening and closing the dialog box:

```
<!DOCTYPE html>
<script src = jquery.js></script>
<script src = jqueryui/js/jquery-ui-1.8.16.custom.min.js></script>

<link rel=stylesheet type=text/css
      href=jqueryui/css/smoothness/jquery-ui-1.8.16.custom.css />

<div id="dialog" title="Window title">
  <p> Content of the dialog box</p>
</div>

<input id=open type=button value=Open>
<input id=close type=button value=Close>

<script>

$("div#dialog").dialog ({
  autoOpen : false
});
```

```
$("#open").click (function (event)     // Open button Treatment
{
  if ($("#dialog").dialog ("isOpen")) alert ("Already open !");
  else $("#dialog").dialog ("open");
});

$("#close").click (function (event)    // Close button Treatment
{
  if (!$("#dialog").dialog ("isOpen")) alert ("Already closed !");
  else $("#dialog").dialog ("close");
});

</script>
```

Initially, the dialog box is created but is not open (options.autoOpen set to false). Before opening the dialog box, we test whether it is already open with dialog ("isOpen"). We do the same for closing it.

Figure 4-5 shows the window after it is opened.

Figure 4-5. Buttons to open and close the dialog box

If you try to open the dialog box a second time, you will receive an alert message that says, "Already open!" (Figure 4-6).

Figure 4-6. An alert message appears when you try to open a dialog box that is already open

Applying an Effect When Opening or Closing the Dialog Box

By default, no effect is used when opening or closing a dialog box. We can apply an effect using the show and hide options (shown in bold). In this example, the dialog box will appear by sliding from the left side of the page (slide effect) and will disappear by enlarging and reducing its opacity (puff effect):

```
<!DOCTYPE html>
<script src = jquery.js></script>
<script src = jqueryui/js/jquery-ui-1.8.16.custom.min.js></script>

<link rel=stylesheet type=text/css
      href=jqueryui/css/smoothness/jquery-ui-1.8.16.custom.css />

<div id="dialog" title="Window title">
  <p> Content of the dialog box</p>
</div>

<script>

$("div#dialog").dialog ({
  show : "slide",
  hide : "puff"
});

</script>
```

Verifying the Closure of the Dialog Box

It is possible to verify the closure of a dialog box with the `options.beforeclose` option. This option corresponds to a method that is activated when the dialog box closes. If the method returns `false`, the dialog box does not close.

In this example, a confirmation message appears when the user tries to close the dialog box (Figure 4-7). The dialog box will be closed when the user clicks the OK button:

```
<!DOCTYPE html>
<script src = jquery.js></script>
<script src = jqueryui/js/jquery-ui-1.8.16.custom.min.js></script>

<link rel=stylesheet type=text/css
      href=jqueryui/css/smoothness/jquery-ui-1.8.16.custom.css />

<div id="dialog" title="Window title">
  <p> Content of the dialog box</p>
</div>

<script>

$("div#dialog").dialog ({
  beforeclose : function (event)
  {
    if (!confirm ("Close dialog ?")) return false;
  }
});

</script>
```

Figure 4-7. The confirmation dialog box verifies closure of the main dialog box

Another way to prevent the closure of the dialog box is to remove the close button. This case is treated in the next section.

Hiding the Close Button

We can prevent the closure of the dialog box by removing (hiding) the close button.

The close button is associated with an `<a>` link with the `ui-dialog-titlebar-close` CSS class. This link can be easily identified in the HTML generated by the call for `dialog (options)` (e.g., with Firebug). It is located in the sibling element before the contents of the dialog box (shown in bold):

```
<!DOCTYPE html>
<script src = jquery.js></script>
<script src = jqueryui/js/jquery-ui-1.8.16.custom.min.js></script>

<link rel=stylesheet type=text/css
      href=jqueryui/css/smoothness/jquery-ui-1.8.16.custom.css />

<div id="dialog" title="Window title">
  <p> Content of the dialog box</p>
</div>

<script>

$("div#dialog").dialog ().prev ().find (".ui-dialog-titlebar-close").hide ();

</script>
```

This statement includes the following:

1. We call `dialog ()` to convert the HTML dialog box.
2. We get the previous sibling of content with `prev ()`.
3. In this relationship, we look for the element with the `ui-dialog-titlebar-close` CSS class.
4. We hide this element using `hide ()`.

This must be done in the listed order. If, for example, we do not call `dialog ()` first, the `prev ()` instruction will not find the link in the previous element, because the HTML has not been turned into a dialog box!

As shown in Figure 4-8, the close button is not visible.

Figure 4-8. Dialog box without a close button

Inserting Buttons in the Dialog Box

We now want to insert buttons in the dialog box, such as Yes and No buttons in a window asking, "Would you like to close the window?" (see Figure 4-9). We can use `options.buttons` (shown in bold) for this.

Users can close the window only by clicking the Yes button—the standard close button has been removed:

```
<!DOCTYPE html>
<script src = jquery.js></script>
<script src = jqueryui/js/jquery-ui-1.8.16.custom.min.js></script>

<link rel=stylesheet type=text/css
      href=jqueryui/css/smoothness/jquery-ui-1.8.16.custom.css />

<div id="dialog" title="Window title">
  <p> Would you like to close the dialog box?</p>
</div>

<script>

$("div#dialog").dialog ({
  buttons : {
    "Yes" : function ()
    {
```

```
        $("div#dialog").dialog ("close");
     },
     "No" : function ()
     {
     }
   }
}).prev().find(".ui-dialog-titlebar-close").hide ();

</script>
```

Figure 4-9. The Yes and No buttons now appear in the dialog box

Inserting Content Using Ajax

Now let's insert content retrieved dynamically from the server into the dialog box before opening. This is done using the `options.open` option (shown in bold). This method is called before the dialog box is displayed:

```
<!DOCTYPE html>
<script src = jquery.js></script>
<script src = jqueryui/js/jquery-ui-1.8.16.custom.min.js></script>

<link rel=stylesheet type=text/css
      href=jqueryui/css/smoothness/jquery-ui-1.8.16.custom.css />

<div id="dialog" title="Window title">
  <p> Content of the dialog box</p>
</div>
```

```
<script>

$("div#dialog").dialog ({
  open : function (event)
  {
    $(this).load ("action.php");
  }
});

</script>
```

Recall that in the event methods (defined here by options.open), the this value represents the HTML element corresponding to the contents of the dialog box. $(this) is a jQuery class object associated with this element of the DOM. The *action.php* file is as follows:

```
<?
  $txt = "<span> Response sent by the server </span>";
  $txt = utf8_encode($txt);
  echo ($txt);
?>
```

The URL of the page displayed in the browser must begin with http://, otherwise the Ajax call cannot be performed.

The content of the dialog box is retrieved by Ajax and the window is displayed with its new content (Figure 4-10).

Figure 4-10. Dialog box initialized dynamically

Changing the Behavior of a Dialog Box with Effects

We have seen that the options used when creating the dialog box can be modified by the `dialog ("option", param, value)` method. The `param` parameter is the name of the option, while the `value` corresponds to its new value.

To illustrate this, let's change the effect for the opening and closing of the window. We'll display two lists for which we can select the desired effect ("puff", "slide", etc.). When creating the dialog box, no effect is associated with it:

```
<!DOCTYPE html>
<script src = jquery.js></script>
<script src = jqueryui/js/jquery-ui-1.8.16.custom.min.js></script>

<link rel=stylesheet type=text/css
     href=jqueryui/css/smoothness/jquery-ui-1.8.16.custom.css />

<div id="dialog" title="Window title">
  <p> Content of the dialog box</p>
</div>

Open effect
<select id=effectopen>
  <option>No effect</option>
  <option>blind</option>
  <option>bounce</option>
  <option>clip</option>
  <option>drop</option>
  <option>fold</option>
  <option>highlight</option>
  <option>puff</option>
  <option>pulsate</option>
  <option>scale</option>
  <option>slide</option>
</select>

<br />

Close effect
<select id=effectclose>
  <option>No effect</option>
  <option>blind</option>
  <option>bounce</option>
  <option>clip</option>
  <option>drop</option>
  <option>fold</option>
  <option>highlight</option>
  <option>puff</option>
  <option>pulsate</option>
  <option>scale</option>
  <option>slide</option>
</select>

<br />
```

```
<input id=open type=button value=Open>

<script>

$("div#dialog").dialog ({
  autoOpen : false
});

$("#effectopen").change (function (event)
{
  var effect = $(this).val ();
  if (effect == "No effect") effect = false;
  $("div#dialog").dialog ("option", "show", effect);
});

$("#effectclose").change (function (event)
{
  var effect = $(this).val ();
  if (effect == "No effect") effect = false;
  $("div#dialog").dialog ("option", "hide", effect);
});

$("#open").click (function (event)
{
  $("#dialog").dialog ("open");
});

</script>
```

Figure 4-11 shows the result with the fold and highlight effects selected.

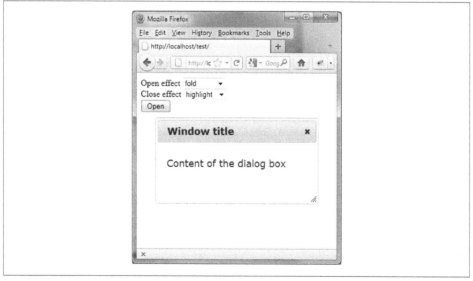

Figure 4-11. Application of an effect at the opening and closing of the dialog box

CHAPTER 5

Buttons

jQuery UI allows us to give a different appearance to interface elements of the HTML page, such as buttons, radio buttons, and checkboxes.

Basic Principles of Buttons

Suppose we want to write the HTML code to display the buttons shown in Figure 5-1.

There are two buttons with a different aspect than the usual buttons. To view them, you must write a `<span>` containing the button text. You can replace the `<span>` element with another HTML element, such as `<div>` or `<button>`, but the button layout will be different (e.g., one above the other for a `<div>`):

```
<!DOCTYPE html>
<script src = jquery.js></script>
<script src = jqueryui/js/jquery-ui-1.8.16.custom.min.js></script>

<link rel=stylesheet type=text/css
      href=jqueryui/css/smoothness/jquery-ui-1.8.16.custom.css />

<span id="button1"> Button 1 </span>
<span id="button2"> Button 2 </span>

<script>

$("#button1, #button2").button ();

</script>
```

The button () method transforms the HTML elements into buttons, with automatic management of mouse movements on them, all managed transparently by jQuery UI.

The `<!DOCTYPE html>` directive is mandatory for improving the display in Internet Explorer.

Figure 5-1. Buttons in the HTML page

Formatting Content

Here, the HTML code that appears after the button () instruction has been changed (Figure 5-2). This code was retrieved using the Firebug extension in Firefox.

```
<!DOCTYPE html>
<html>
  <head>
  <body>
    <span id="button1" class="ui-button ui-widget ui-state-default
      ui-corner-all ui-button-text-only" role="button">
        <span class="ui-button-text"> Button 1 </span>
    </span>
    <span id="button2" class="ui-button ui-widget ui-state-default
      ui-corner-all ui-button-text-only" role="button">
        <span class="ui-button-text"> Button 2 </span>
    </span>
    <script>
  </body>
</html>
```

Figure 5-2. HTML generated by the button () method

Again, as with other functions of jQuery UI, it is possible to use the CSS classes to customize the display of elements. For example, if we change the ui-button CSS class associated with <span> elements, we get a new appearance for the buttons (as shown in Figure 5-3).

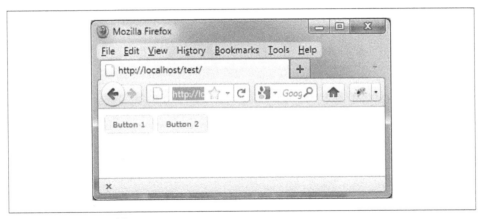

Figure 5-3. Customized buttons

Modify these elements (shown in bold) in the HTML by adding a `<style>` tag:

```
<!DOCTYPE html>
<script src = jquery.js></script>
<script src = jqueryui/js/jquery-ui-1.8.16.custom.min.js></script>

<link rel=stylesheet type=text/css
      href=jqueryui/css/smoothness/jquery-ui-1.8.16.custom.css />

<style type=text/css>
  span.ui-button {
    font-size : 10px;
  }

</style>

<span id="button1"> Button 1 </span>
<span id="button2"> Button 2 </span>

<script>

$("#button1, #button2").button ();

</script>
```

This HTML code is identical, except that we added the `<style>` tag after the inclusion of jQuery UI styles. The addition of our own styles must be done after those of jQuery UI, otherwise our changes will be ignored.

The button () Method

The button () method can be used in two forms:

- $(selector, context).button (options);
- $(selector, context).button ("action", params);

The button (options) Method

The button (options) method declares that an HTML element should be managed as a button. The options parameter is an object that specifies the appearance and behavior of the button.

A button can be represented by text, but can also be associated with icons that are predefined in a jQuery UI CSS file associated with each theme (here, the *jquery.ui.theme.css* file). This file contains a set of CSS classes to access the icons located in a file in the *jqueryui/development-bundle/themes/smoothness/images* directory (for the smoothness theme). In this CSS file, you will see the CSS class definitions, such as the following:

```
CSS class definition associated with an icon in the images file
.ui-icon-calendar { background-position: -32px -112px; }
```

This allows us to use the ui-calendar-icon class in a button, for example, to use a calendar icon for the button.

The icons available in jQuery UI are shown in Figure 5-4.

Figure 5-4. Available icons in jQuery UI

Table 5-1 describes the options for managing buttons.

Table 5-1. Options for managing buttons

Option	Function
options.disabled	When set to true, the button will appear inactive. Mouseovers will have no effect, but clicks on the button will continue to be taken into account.
options.label	Corresponds to the text displayed in the button. If not specified, the contents of the HTML element are used as button text.
options.icons	Associates icons with the button. There may be one before the button text (primary icon) and after (secondary icon). The values of the primary and secondary properties are the names of the CSS class defined in the CSS file (e.g., "ui-icon-calendar").
options.text	Indicates whether the button text should be displayed. When set to false, the text will not be displayed. In this case, at least one icon should be present.

The button ("action", params) Method

The button ("action", params) method allows an action on buttons, such as disabling or changing the button text. The action is specified as a string in the first argument (e.g., "disable" to disable a button). Table 5-2 describes the actions for this method.

Table 5-2. The button ("action", params) method actions

Action	Function
button ("disable")	Disable the button.
button ("enable")	Enable the button.
button ("refresh")	Refresh the display of the button. This is useful when the buttons are handled by the program and the display does not necessarily correspond to the internal state.
button ("option", param)	Retrieve the value of the option specified in param. This option is one of those used in button (options).
button ("option", param, value)	Change the value of the param option. This option is one of those used in button (options).
button ("destroy")	Remove the management of the buttons. The buttons revert to simple HTML without CSS class or event management.

Event Handling on Buttons with bind ()

jQuery UI has not added new events associated with buttons. Indeed, the management of the mouse actions corresponds to existing events (click, mouseover, etc.) used as usual by jQuery with the bind () method.

Radio Buttons

jQuery UI can manage radio buttons so that they have the appearance of the buttons above.

Displaying Radio Buttons

The HTML code you write for this is somewhat less flexible than the code used so far. We must only use an `<input>` element to represent a radio button, in which the text associated with the radio button will take the form of a `<label>` tag.

For example, to display two radio buttons to choose the sex of a person, as shown in Figures 5-5 and 5-6, we write the HTML code as follows:

```
<!DOCTYPE html>
<script src = jquery.js></script>
<script src = jqueryui/js/jquery-ui-1.8.16.custom.min.js></script>

<link rel=stylesheet type=text/css
      href=jqueryui/css/smoothness/jquery-ui-1.8.16.custom.css />

Sex : <input type=radio name=sex id=m><label for=m>Male</label></input>
      <input type=radio name=sex id=f><label for=f>Female</label></input>

<script>

$("input").button ();

</script>
```

Notice the use of the for attribute in the `<label>` tag to associate the text with the radio button. If you forget to add this part, the selection and deselection of the buttons no longer takes place.

Figure 5-5. Radio buttons, where neither is selected

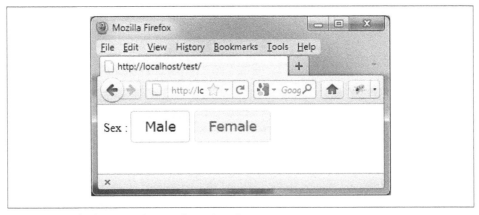

Figure 5-6. Radio buttons, where Male is selected

Improving the Display with buttonset ()

The radio buttons shown in Figures 5-5 and 5-6, are certainly more visually pleasing than the traditional radio buttons, but it would be better to organize them to show that they form a block. We can do this by slightly modifying the HTML code with the changes shown in bold:

```
<!DOCTYPE html>
<script src = jquery.js></script>
<script src = jqueryui/js/jquery-ui-1.8.16.custom.min.js></script>

<link rel=stylesheet type=text/css
      href=jqueryui/css/smoothness/jquery-ui-1.8.16.custom.css />

<div>
  Sex : <input type=radio name=sex id=m><label for=m>Male</label></input>
        <input type=radio name=sex id=f><label for=f>Female</label></input>
</div>

<script>

$("input").button ();
$("div").buttonset ();

</script>
```

The difference from the previous code is that we have wrapped <input> elements into a <div>, to which we applied the jQuery UI buttonset () method to make the buttons look like a single block. The display of the buttons is different, but the behavior remains the same.

The result of this script is shown in Figure 5-7.

Figure 5-7. Radio buttons now form a single block

Checkboxes

The appearance of the checkboxes is the same as radio buttons, but it is possible to select and deselect each checkbox independently (see Figure 5-8).

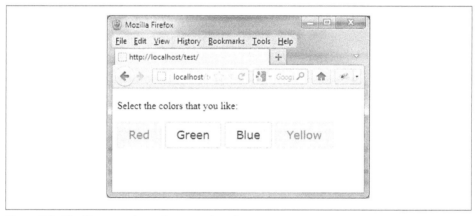

Figure 5-8. Checkboxes with two buttons selected

Displaying Checkboxes

To display the checkboxes, change the `type` attribute of `<input>` elements, replacing radio with checkbox:

```
<!DOCTYPE html>
<script src = jquery.js></script>
<script src = jqueryui/js/jquery-ui-1.8.16.custom.min.js></script>
<link rel=stylesheet type=text/css
      href=jqueryui/css/smoothness/jquery-ui-1.8.16.custom.css />
```

```
<p>Select the colors that you like:</p>
<input type=checkbox name=red id=idred><label for=idred>Red</label></input>
<input type=checkbox name=green id=idgreen><label for=idgreen>Green</label></input>
<input type=checkbox name=blue id=idblue><label for=idblue>Blue</label></input>
<input type=checkbox name=yellow id=idyellow><label for=idyellow>Yellow</label></
input>
<script>
$("input").button ();
</script>
```

Improving the Display with buttonset ()

We can also improve the display by combining checkboxes into a block:

```
<!DOCTYPE html>
<script src = jquery.js></script>
<script src = jqueryui/js/jquery-ui-1.8.16.custom.min.js></script>
<link rel=stylesheet type=text/css
      href=jqueryui/css/smoothness/jquery-ui-1.8.16.custom.css />
<p>Select the colors that you like:</p>
<div>
  <input type=checkbox name=red id=idred><label for=idred>Red</label></input>
  <input type=checkbox name=green id=idgreen><label for=idgreen>Green</label></input>
  <input type=checkbox name=blue id=idblue><label for=idblue>Blue</label></input>
  <input type=checkbox name=yellow id=idyellow><label for=idyellow>Yellow</label></
input>
</div>
<script>
$("input").button ();
$("div").buttonset ();
</script>
```

We observe here the same principle as the radio buttons. This is jQuery UI, which manages the buttons differently due to **type** attributes of **<input>** elements. The display is different, but the behavior is the same (Figure 5-9).

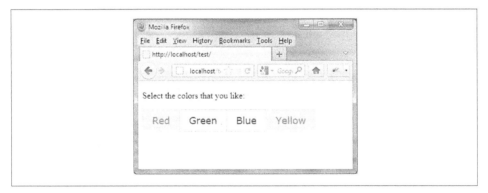

Figure 5-9. Checkboxes in a block

Examples of Using Buttons

Here are some examples that apply the principles discussed in this chapter.

Displaying Icons in Buttons

The `options.icons` option defines an icon for the button. For example, to define a volume button, including the volume icon, as shown in Figure 5-10, write the following basic code (shown in bold):

```
<!DOCTYPE html>
<script src = jquery.js></script>
<script src = jqueryui/js/jquery-ui-1.8.16.custom.min.js></script>

<link rel=stylesheet type=text/css
      href=jqueryui/css/smoothness/jquery-ui-1.8.16.custom.css />

<span id=volume>Volume</span>

<script>

$("#volume").button ({
  icons : { secondary : "ui-icon-volume-off" }
});

</script>
```

The icon is inserted after the text (`secondary` property). About the `"ui-icon-volume-off"` value is that used in the CSS styles of jQuery UI for the volume icon (Figure 5-10).

Figure 5-10. Icon inserted after the text on a button

You can change the appearance of the button when clicked to visually convey that a button has been turned on or off. For example, in Figure 5-11, we see an icon showing that the volume is turned on:

```
<!DOCTYPE html>
<script src = jquery.js></script>
<script src = jqueryui/js/jquery-ui-1.8.16.custom.min.js></script>

<link rel=stylesheet type=text/css
      href=jqueryui/css/smoothness/jquery-ui-1.8.16.custom.css />

<span id=volume>Volume</span>

<script>

$("#volume").button ({
  icons : { secondary : "ui-icon-volume-off" }
}).click (function (event)
{
  // current volume
  var volume = $(this).button ("option", "icons").secondary ==
                    "ui-icon-volume-off" ? false : true;

  // we reverse the volume (On / Off)
  if (volume) $(this).button ("option", "icons",
                              { secondary : "ui-icon-volume-off" });
  else $(this).button ("option", "icons", { secondary : "ui-icon-volume-on" });
});

</script>
```

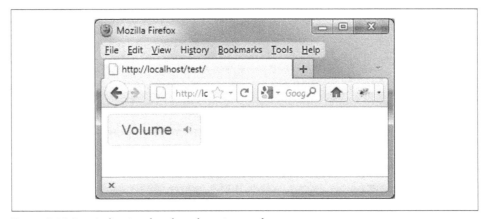

Figure 5-11. Icon indicating that the volume is turned on

Let's also change the button text to display the text Volume On or Volume Off in addition to changing the icon:

```
<!DOCTYPE html>
<script src = jquery.js></script>
<script src = jqueryui/js/jquery-ui-1.8.16.custom.min.js></script>

<link rel=stylesheet type=text/css
      href=jqueryui/css/smoothness/jquery-ui-1.8.16.custom.css />
```

```
<span id=volume>Volume Off</span>

<script>

$("#volume").button ({
  icons : { secondary : "ui-icon-volume-off" }
}).click (function (event)
{
  // current volume
  var volume = $(this).button ("option", "icons").secondary ==
                    "ui-icon-volume-off" ? false : true;

  // we reverse the volume (On / Off)
  if (volume)
  {
    // text
    $(this).button ("option", "label", "Volume Off");
    // icon
    $(this).button ("option", "icons", { secondary : "ui-icon-volume-off" });
  }
  else
  {
    // text
    $(this).button ("option", "label", "Volume On");
    // icon
    $(this).button ("option", "icons", { secondary : "ui-icon-volume-on" });
  }
});

</script>
```

At launch, the volume is off (Figure 5-12), and it is enabled (on) when users click the button (Figure 5-13).

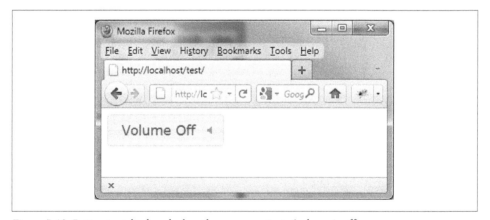

Figure 5-12. Button text displayed when the program starts (volume is off)

Figure 5-13. Button text after clicking (volume is turned on)

Creating a Calculator

We can use buttons to create a calculator like the one shown in Figure 5-14. It can perform the four basic operations, and users can reset the display by clicking the button associated with the display of the result (at the top of the window).

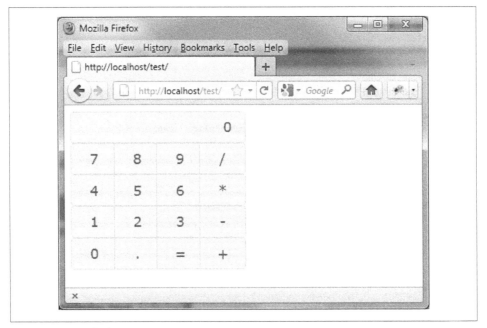

Figure 5-14. A calculator

Basic program

Use the following script to create a basic calculator:

```html
<!DOCTYPE html>
<script src = jquery.js></script>
<script src = jqueryui/js/jquery-ui-1.8.16.custom.min.js></script>

<link rel=stylesheet type=text/css
      href=jqueryui/css/smoothness/jquery-ui-1.8.16.custom.css />

<style type=text/css>
  span.ui-button-text-only {      /* any key */
    width : 60px;
  }
  div.ui-button-text-only {       /* field result */
    width : 230px;
    text-align : right;
  }
  div.ui-button-text-only.ie {    /* field of IE specific result */
    width : 230px;
  }
</style>

<div id=result>0</div>

<div class=touches>
  <span>7</span><span>8</span><span>9</span><span>/</span>
</div>
<div class=touches>
  <span>4</span><span>5</span><span>6</span><span>*</span>
</div>
<div class=touches>
  <span>1</span><span>2</span><span>3</span><span>-</span>
</div>
<div class=touches>
  <span>0</span><span>.</span><span>=</span><span>+</span>
</div>

<script>

var result = 0;          // calculation result
var previous_touche;     // previously pressed key
var last_operation;      // last operation

$("span").button ().click (function (event)
{
  var touche = $(this).text ();           // button currently pressed
  var display = $("#result").text ();     // current display (string)
  if (touche == "+" || touche == "-" ||
     touche == "*" || touche == "/" ||
     touche == "=")
  {
    if (previous_touche != "+" && previous_touche != "-" &&
        previous_touche != "*" && previous_touche != "/")
    {
```

```javascript
      // we pressed +, -, *, / or = :
      // if a previous operation was in progress, it performs
      if (last_operation == "+")
      {
        result += parseFloat (display);
        $("#result span").text (format_display (result));
      }
      else if (last_operation == "-")
      {
        result -= parseFloat (display);
        $("#result span").text (format_display (result));
      }
      else if (last_operation == "*")
      {
        result *= parseFloat (display);
        $("#result span").text (format_display (result));
      }
      else if (last_operation == "/")
      {
        result /= parseFloat (display);
        $("#result span").text (format_display (result));
      }
      result = parseFloat ($("#result").text ());
    }
    if (touche == "=") last_operation = undefined;
    else last_operation = touche;
  }
  else
  {
    // we pressed a number or point
    // we combine this key with the current display,
    // unless the previous button was a sign operation
    if (display == "0" ||
        previous_touche == "+" ||
        previous_touche == "-" ||
        previous_touche == "*" ||
        previous_touche == "/" ||
        previous_touche == "=") display = "";
    if (display.length < 16) display += touche;
    $("#result span").text (display);
  }
  previous_touche = touche;
});

$("div.touches").buttonset ();

$("div#result").button ().click (function (event)
{
  // click on the result field: it sets the display to 0
  var display = $("#result").text ();
  if (display == "0") result = 0;
  $("#result span").text ("0");
});

// consider a special style for Internet Explorer
```

```
if ($.browser.msie) $("div#result").addClass ("ie");

// ensure that the displayed result is not more than 16 characters
function format_display (display)
{
  display += "";
  if (display.length < 16) return display;
  if (display.match (/\./)) return display.substring (0, 15);
  else return ("Out of Memory");
}

</script>
```

This program includes the management of keys (e.g., retaining information about which button was clicked and whether to perform a calculation or not).

To account for differences in display between Internet Explorer and other browsers, the display field of the result has an `ie` CSS class that is used automatically if jQuery detects this browser.

This calculator currently runs in the browser window. With a few additions, we can turn the calculator into an application that runs separately from the main browser window. For this, we can create a jQuery plug-in.

Improving the program

Rather than creating a standalone calculator application, let's create a calculator plug-in. The calculator will be presented as a dialog box that opens on top of the page elements when displayed (Figure 5-15). This will simplify the code of our program by outsourcing all of the calculator code to a third-party file that can be reused for other applications.

Here we have a main program with a Display calculator button, which calls the corresponding plug-in when clicked. The calculator is displayed on top of the page elements in a centered position. Users can close it by clicking the close button in the top right corner of the dialog box.

The program below displays the button using the calculator:

```
<!DOCTYPE html>
<script src = jquery.js></script>
<script src = jqueryui/js/jquery-ui-1.8.16.custom.min.js></script>
<script src = jquery.calculator.js></script>

<link rel=stylesheet type=text/css
      href=jqueryui/css/smoothness/jquery-ui-1.8.16.custom.css />
<link rel=stylesheet type=text/css href=jquery.calculator.css />

<button onclick=$.calculator()>Display calculator </button>
```

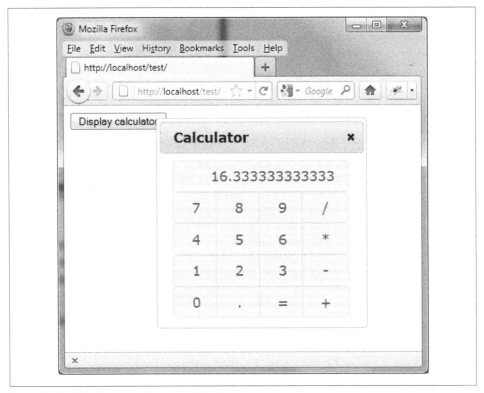

Figure 5-15. Calculator opening as a dialog box

This simple code displays a button where the treatment of the onclick event calls the calculator () plug-in. The functionality of plug-in matches a JavaScript *jquery.calculator.js* file and a *jquery.calculator.css* CSS file, both included in the HTML page:

```
span.ui-button-text-only {      /* any key */
  width : 60px;
}
div.ui-button-text-only {       /* field result */
  width : 230px;
  text-align : right;
}
div.ui-button-text-only.ie {   /* field of IE specific result */
  width : 230px;
}
```

We just put the CSS styles in an external file, which will be included in the main HTML file.

The plug-in file is jquery.calculator.js, containing the following lines:

```
(function ($)
{
  $.calculator = function ()
```

```
{
  var result = 0;         // calculation result
  var previous_touche;    // previously pressed key
  var last_operation;     // last operation

  if ($("#calculator").length)
  {
    // calculator has been already created, simply display
    $("#calculator").dialog ("open");
    return;
  }

  // creation of the calculator, only on the first call of the function
  var html = "<div id=calculator> \
                 <div id=result>0</div> \
                 <div class=touches> \
                    <span>7</span><span>8</span><span>9</span><span>/</span> \
                 </div> \
                 <div class=touches> \
                    <span>4</span><span>5</span><span>6</span><span>*</span> \
                 </div> \
                 <div class=touches> \
                    <span>1</span><span>2</span><span>3</span><span>-</span> \
                 </div> \
                 <div class=touches> \
                    <span>0</span><span>.</span><span>=</span><span>+</span> \
                 </div> \
              </div>"

  $(html).appendTo ("body");

  $("#calculator div.touches span").button ().click (function (event)
  {
    var touche = $(this).text ();        // button currently pressed
    var display = $("#result").text ();  // current view (string)
    if (touche == "+" || touche == "-" ||
        touche == "*" || touche == "/" ||
        touche == "=")
    {
      if (previous_touche != "+" && previous_touche != "-" &&
          previous_touche != "*" && previous_touche != "/")
      {
        // we pressed +, -, *, / or = :
        // if a previous operation was in progress, it performs
        if (last_operation == "+")
        {
          result += parseFloat (display);
          $("#result span").text (format_display (result));
        }
        else if (last_operation == "-")
        {
          result -= parseFloat (display);
          $("#result span").text (format_display (result));
        }
        else if (last_operation == "*")
```

```
      {
        result *= parseFloat (display);
        $("#result span").text (format_display (result));
      }
      else if (last_operation == "/")
      {
        result /= parseFloat (display);
        $("#result span").text (format_display (result));
      }
      result = parseFloat ($("#result").text ());
    }
    if (touche == "=") last_operation = undefined;
    else last_operation = touche;
  }
  else
  {
    // we pressed a number or point
    // we combine this key with the current display,
    // unless the previous button was a sign operation
    if (display == "0" ||
        previous_touche == "+" ||
        previous_touche == "-" ||
        previous_touche == "*" ||
        previous_touche == "/" ||
        previous_touche == "=") display = "";
    if (display.length < 16) display += touche;
    $("#result span").text (display);
  }
  previous_touche = touche;
});

$("#calculator div.touches").buttonset ();

$("#calculator div#result").button ().click (function (event)
{
  // click on the result field: it sets the display to 0
  var display = $("#calculator #result").text ();
  if (display == "0") result = 0;
  $("#calculator #result span").text ("0");
});

// consider a special style for Internet Explorer
if ($.browser.msie) $("#calculator div#result").addClass ("ie");

// creation of the window with the calculator
$("#calculator").dialog ({
  title : "Calculator",
  resizable : false,
  width : $.browser.msie ? 275 : 270
});

// ensure that the displayed result is not more than 16 characters
function format_display (display)
{
  display += "";
```

```
        if (display.length < 16) return display;
        if (display.match (/\./)) return display.substring (0, 15);
        else return ("Out of Memory");
    }
  }
}) (jQuery);
```

This program is almost identical to the previous, except that the HTML code of the calculator is created in the JavaScript plug-in. In addition, we added the dialog box containing the calculator.

CHAPTER 6

Progress Bars

Progress bars allow you to view the progress of a task, such as transferring a file. jQuery UI can handle them easily.

Basic Principles of Progress Bars

Suppose we want to write the HTML code to display the progress bar shown in Figure 6-1. This is a container that will gradually fill in to indicate the progress of a task (for the moment, it is almost empty and will start to fill in from the left side).

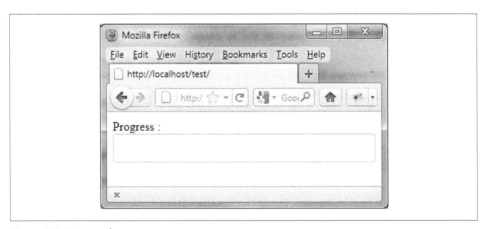

Figure 6-1. Progress bar

As required by jQuery UI, we represent the progress bar with a `<div>` element (shown in bold):

```
<script src = jquery.js></script>
<script src = jqueryui/js/jquery-ui-1.8.16.custom.min.js></script>

<link rel=stylesheet type=text/css
      href=jqueryui/css/smoothness/jquery-ui-1.8.16.custom.css />
```

```
Progress : <div id=progressbar></div>

<script>

$("div#progressbar").progressbar ();

</script>
```

This indicates that each <div> element corresponding to the progress bar is managed by the jQuery UI progressbar () method.

Formatting Content

Figure 6-2 shows an example of the HTML generated by jQuery UI once modified by the progressbar () instruction (this code was recovered using the Firebug extension in Firefox).

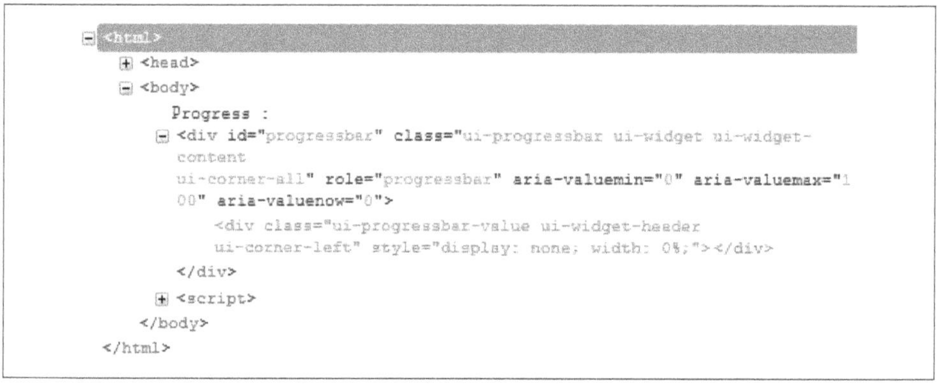

Figure 6-2. HTML code generated by the progressbar () method

Again, it is possible to use CSS classes of elements to customize the display. For example, if we change the ui-progressbar CSS class associated with <div> elements, we get a new appearance for progress bars, such as that shown in Figure 6-3, with a height of 10 pixels:

```
<script src = jquery.js></script>
<script src = jqueryui/js/jquery-ui-1.8.16.custom.min.js></script>

<link rel=stylesheet type=text/css
      href=jqueryui/css/smoothness/jquery-ui-1.8.16.custom.css />

<style type=text/css>
  div#progressbar.ui-progressbar {
    height : 10px;
  }
</style>
```

```
Progress : <div id=progressbar></div>

<script>

$("div#progressbar").progressbar ();

</script>
```

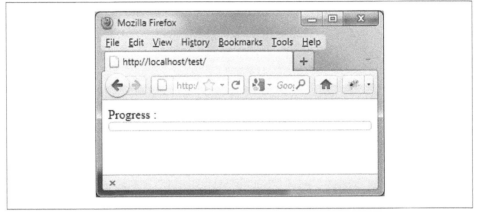

Figure 6-3. Customized progress bar

The progressbar () Method

The progressbar () method can be used in two forms:

- $(selector, context).progressbar (options)
- $(selector, context).progressbar ("action", params)

The progressbar (options) Method

The progressbar (options) method declares that an HTML element should be managed in the form of a progress bar. The options parameter is an object that specifies the appearance and behavior of the progress bar. The available options (described in Table 6-1) allow you to manage the progress bars or events taking place in the progress bar.

Table 6-1. Options for managing progress bars and events

Option	Function
options.value	Percentage of the progress bar to fill (from 0 to 100).
options.change	The change (event) method is called whenever the fill percentage of the progress bar changes (by changing the options.value option).

The progressbar ("action", params) Method

The `progressbar ("action", params)` method can perform an action on the progress bar, such as changing the percentage filled. The action is specified as a string in the first argument (e.g., `"value"` to change the percentage filled). The options for this method are described in Table 6-2.

Table 6-2. The progressbar ("action", params) method actions

Action	Function
progressbar ("value")	Retrieve the current value of `options.value`, that is, the percentage of fill in the progress bar.
progressbar ("value", value)	Specify a new `value` to the percentage filled in the progress bar.
progressbar ("option", param)	Retrieve the value of the `param` option specified. This option corresponds to one of those used in `progressbar (options)`.
progressbar ("option", param, value)	Change the `value` of the `param` option. This option corresponds to one of those used in `progressbar (options)`.
progressbar ("destroy")	Remove the management of progress bars. Progress bars revert to simple HTML without CSS class or event management.

Handling Events in Progress Bars with bind ()

In addition to event methods used through the options offered by the `progressbar (options)` method, jQuery UI allows us to manage these events using the `bind ()` method.

To do this, jQuery UI includes the `progressbarchange` event, which has the same meaning as the `options.change` option.

Examples of Using Progress Bars

This section includes examples of different ways to use progress bars.

Incrementing a Progress Bar

Here is a typical use of progress bars. We use a counter (timer) to steadily increment the percentage of fill in the progress bar:

```
<script src = jquery.js></script>
<script src = jqueryui/js/jquery-ui-1.8.16.custom.min.js></script>

<link rel=stylesheet type=text/css
      href=jqueryui/css/smoothness/jquery-ui-1.8.16.custom.css />

Progress : <div id=progressbar></div>
```

```
<script>

$("div#progressbar").progressbar ();

var value = 0;
var timer = setInterval (function ()
{
  $("div#progressbar").progressbar ("value", value);
  value++;
  if (value > 100) clearInterval (timer);
}, 10);

</script>
```

The callback function specified in setInterval (delay, callback) is called at the end of each specified time period (here, every 10 milliseconds). clearInterval (timer) prevents this callback function from being called once the percentage reaches its maximum value of 100 (Figure 6-4).

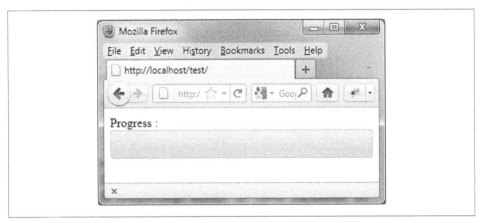

Figure 6-4. The progress bar is completely filled

Performing Processing at Different Stages of Completion

In addition to incrementing the progress bar, it is possible to perform processing at particular stages of completion. Let's use this functionality to update a numerical display of percent complete every time there is a change in the percent filled (shown in Figure 6-5). This is done using options.change, which notifies of any change in the value of the progress bar fill.

```
<script src = jquery.js></script>
<script src = jqueryui/js/jquery-ui-1.8.16.custom.min.js></script>

<link rel=stylesheet type=text/css
      href=jqueryui/css/smoothness/jquery-ui-1.8.16.custom.css />

Progress : <div id=progressbar></div>
```

```
<div id=percent style=text-align:center>0</div>

<script>

$("div#progressbar").progressbar ({
  change : function (event)
  {
    var value = $("div#progressbar").progressbar ("value");
    $("#percent").html (value + " %");
  }
});

var value = 0;
var timer = setInterval (function ()
{
  $("div#progressbar").progressbar ("value", value);
  value++;
  if (value > 100) clearInterval (timer);
}, 10);

</script>
```

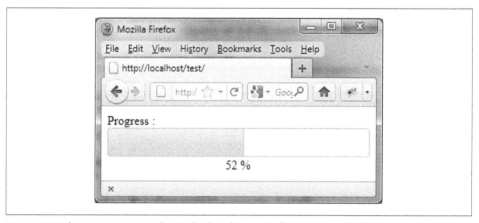

Figure 6-5. The percentage complete is displayed numerically

CHAPTER 7

Sliders

Sliders are widgets that allow users to change the numerical value of data by moving a cursor on a graduated axis. For example, a graduated slider from 18 to 100 can allow users to select age graphically rather than entering it manually in an input field.

Basic Principles of Sliders

To display a slider like the one shown in Figure 7-1, we write the following HTML code, followed once again by a call to the jQuery UI method, which manages this type of graphical component:

```
<!DOCTYPE html>
<script src = jquery.js></script>
<script src = jqueryui/js/jquery-ui-1.8.16.custom.min.js></script>

<link rel=stylesheet type=text/css
      href=jqueryui/css/smoothness/jquery-ui-1.8.16.custom.css />

<h3>Slider</h3>
<div id=slider></div>

<script>

$("div#slider").slider ();

</script>
```

The slider (axis and cursor) is represented by a <div> element (with slider ID).

A <script> tag is added to indicate that each <div> corresponding to a slider is managed by the slider () method.

The operation of a slider is simple: you can move the cursor on its axis either by dragging it with the mouse (drag-and-drop mechanism) or by clicking on a point on the axis. In both cases, the cursor moves to the indicated location.

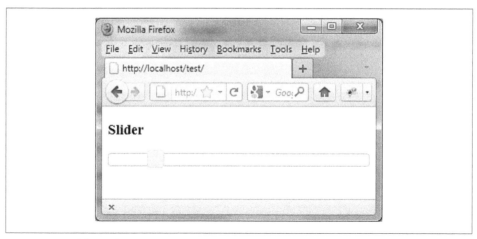

Figure 7-1. A slider in the HTML page

Formatting Content

The use of the `slider ()` method changes the appearance of HTML elements in the page, adding new CSS classes that give them the appropriate style.

Figure 7-2 shows the HTML generated by jQuery UI, once the `slider ()` instruction modifies the HTML (the code was recovered using the Firebug extension in Firefox).

```
<!DOCTYPE html>
<html>
  <head>
  <body>
      <h3> Slider </h3>
      <div id="slider" class="ui-slider ui-slider-horizontal ui-widget
         ui-widget-content ui-corner-all">
          <a class="ui-slider-handle ui-state-default
             ui-corner-all" href="#" style="left: 9%;"></a>
      </div>
      <script>
  </body>
</html>
```

Figure 7-2. HTML generated by the slider () method

CSS classes of elements customize the display. For example, if we change the `ui-slider` class associated with `<div>` elements using a `<style>` tag, as in the following HTML code, we can change the slider's width and background color:

```
<!DOCTYPE html>
<script src = jquery.js></script>
<script src = jqueryui/js/jquery-ui-1.8.16.custom.min.js></script>
```

```
<link rel=stylesheet type=text/css
      href=jqueryui/css/smoothness/jquery-ui-1.8.16.custom.css />

<style type=text/css>
  div#slider.ui-slider {
    width : 100px;
    background : black;
  }
</style>

<h3>Slider</h3>
<div id=slider></div>

<script>

$("div#slider").slider ();

</script>
```

This HTML code is identical, except that we added the `<style>` tag after the inclusion of jQuery UI styles. The addition of our own styles must be done after those of jQuery UI, or our changes will be ignored. Figure 7-3 shows the new style.

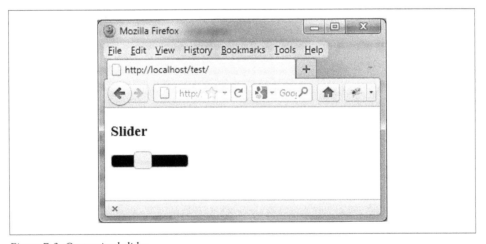

Figure 7-3. Customized slider

The slider now has a width of 100 pixels and a black background.

The slider () Method

The `slider ()` method can be used in two forms:

- `$(selector, context).slider (options)`
- `$(selector, context).slider ("action", params)`

The slider (options) Method

The `slider (options)` method declares that an HTML element should be managed as a slider. The `options` parameter is an object that specifies the appearance and behavior of the slider.

Some options allow you to position multiple cursors on the axis and specify whether the cursors can pass each other on the axis.

Managing the appearance and behavior of sliders

Table 7-1 describes the options for managing the appearance and behavior of sliders.

Table 7-1. Options for managing slider appearance and behavior

Option	Function
options.disabled	If `true`, disables the slider. No cursor movement or click on the axis will be considered until the slider is returned to the enabled state (by `slider ("enable")`).
options.animate	If `true`, creates an animated effect when users click directly on the axis. By default, it is set to `false`, in which case clicking on the axis places the cursor directly where the user clicked, with no animated effect.
options.orientation	Indicates the horizontal or vertical orientation of the slider. The default value is `"horizontal"`. To position the slider vertically, use `"vertical"`.

Managing the values of cursors

Table 7-2 describes the options available for managing the values that appear on the slider.

Table 7-2. Options for managing slider values

Option	Function
options.min	Indicates the value of the cursor when positioned at the beginning of the axis (first graduation). The default is 0.
options.max	Indicates the value of the cursor when positioned at the end of the axis (last graduation). The default is 100.
options.value	Indicates the value of the cursor in the [`options.min, options.max`] interval.
options.values	When using multiple cursors, indicates the value of these in an array. The number of values is the number of cursors used.
options.range	When set to `true`, indicates that two cursors should be used (`options.values` should have a length of 2, with each value indicating the initial value for a cursor).
	If `"min"` or `"max"`, a single cursor must be used (if not, this option does not work). In all cases, the space between the two cursors on the axis is styled (if `true`), or the space between the cursor and the beginning of the axis (if `"min"`) or the space between the cursor and the end of the axis (if `"max"`).
options.step	Indicates the increment of displacement of a cursor on the axis. The default is 1.

Managing events on the slider

The events listed in Table 7-3 are generated by either clicks on the cursor, clicks on the axis, or calls to the `slider ("value", value)` or `slider ("values", index, value)` methods.

Table 7-3. Options for managing events on a slider

Option	Function
options.start	The start (event) method is called when the movement of a cursor starts.
options.stop	The stop (event) method is called when the movement of a cursor finishes.
options.change	The change (event) method is called when the movement of a cursor finishes (same as options.stop).
options.slide	The slide (event) method is called when the cursor is moved using drag-and-drop. This method is not called when users click directly on the axis.

The slider ("action", params) Method

The `slider ("action", params)` method (detailed in Table 7-4) allows an action on the slider, such as moving the cursor to a new location. The action is specified as a string in the first argument (e.g., `"value"` to indicate a new value of the cursor).

Table 7-4. The slider ("action", params) method actions

Action	Function
slider ("disable")	Disable the functioning of the slider. Clicks will not be taken into account.
slider ("enable")	Reactivate the functioning of the slider. The clicks are again considered.
slider ("value")	Retrieve the current value of options.value (the indicator). Use only if the indicator is unique (if not, use slider ("values")).
slider ("value", value)	Change the value of the indicator. Use only if the indicator is unique (otherwise use slider ("values", values)).
slider ("values")	Retrieve the current value of options.values (the value of the indicators in an array).
slider ("values", values)	Assign new values to the indicators in an array.
slider ("option", param)	Retrieve the value of the specified param option. This option corresponds to one of those used with slider (options).
slider ("option", param, value)	Change the value of the param option. This option corresponds to one of those used with slider (options).
slider ("destroy")	Remove the management of the sliders. Sliders revert to simple HTML without CSS class or event management.

Event Management on the Sliders with bind ()

In addition to event methods in the options of the slider (options) method, jQuery UI allows us to manage these events using the bind () method (described in Table 7-5).

Table 7-5. Types of events created by jQuery UI

Event	Function
slidestart	Same meaning as options.start.
slidestop	Same meaning as options.stop.
slidechange	Same meaning as options.change.
slide	Same meaning as options.slide.

Examples of Using Sliders

Let's put our knowledge of sliders to use with some basic examples. In this section, we'll write script that creates and manages one or multiple sliders.

Displaying the Value of One Indicator

Let's start with a single indicator that displays the value when start, stop, slide, and change events occur.

We first get the value of the indicator at each event, then we display it in the field for the event. This allows us to see when each event is triggered by jQuery UI:

```
<!DOCTYPE html>
<script src = jquery.js></script>
<script src = jqueryui/js/jquery-ui-1.8.16.custom.min.js></script>

<link rel=stylesheet type=text/css
      href=jqueryui/css/smoothness/jquery-ui-1.8.16.custom.css />

<h3> Slider </h3>
<div id=slider></div><br />
Start : <span id=valuestart></span><br />
Stop : <span id=valuestop></span><br />
Change : <span id=valuechange></span><br />
Slide : <span id=valueslide></span>

<script>

$("div#slider").slider ({
  animate : true,
  start : function (event)
  {
    var value = $("div#slider").slider ("value");
    $("#valuestart").html (value);
  },
```

```
    stop : function (event)
    {
      var value = $("div#slider").slider ("value");
      $("#valuestop").html (value);
    },
    change : function (event)
    {
      var value = $("div#slider").slider ("value");
      $("#valuechange").html (value);
    },
    slide : function (event)
    {
      var value = $("div#slider").slider ("value");
      $("#valueslide").html (value);
    }
  });
```

```
</script>
```

The result of this script is shown in Figure 7-4.

Figure 7-4. Displaying the value of an indicator on the slider

This example takes into account the display of a single slider, but jQuery UI can use several simultaneously, as discussed in the following section.

Displaying the Values of Two Indicators

Let's use two cursors that display values for each event. The program is almost identical to the previous, except that options.range is set to true and the values of the indicators are retrieved by the slider ("values") method.

Positioning `options.range` to `true` allows us to modify the appearance of the space between the two indicators on the axis (the default is a gray background):

```
<!DOCTYPE html>
<script src = jquery.js></script>
<script src = jqueryui/js/jquery-ui-1.8.16.custom.min.js></script>

<link rel=stylesheet type=text/css
      href=jqueryui/css/smoothness/jquery-ui-1.8.16.custom.css />

<h3> Slider </h3>
<div id=slider></div><br />
Start : <span id=valuestart></span><br />
Stop : <span id=valuestop></span><br />
Change : <span id=valuechange></span><br />
Slide : <span id=valueslide></span>

<script>

$("div#slider").slider ({
  animate : true,
  range : true,
  values : [0, 0],   // initial values of cursors
  start : function (event)
  {
    var values = $("div#slider").slider ("values");
    $("#valuestart").html (values[0] + ", " + values[1]);
  },
  stop : function (event)
  {
    var values = $("div#slider").slider ("values");
    $("#valuestop").html (values[0] + ", " + values[1]);
  },
  change : function (event)
  {
    var values = $("div#slider").slider ("values");
    $("#valuechange").html (values[0] + ", " + values[1]);
  },
  slide : function (event)
  {
    var values = $("div#slider").slider ("values");
    $("#valueslide").html (values[0] + ", " + values[1]);
  }
});

</script>
```

The result of this script is shown in Figure 7-5.

Figure 7-5. Displaying the values of two indicators on the slider

Adjusting the Opacity of an Image Using a Slider

Here is a concrete example of using a slider to change the opacity of an image (Figure 7-6). The opacity can vary from 0 to 1. On startup, it is 1, so the cursor should be at its maximum level.

The value of the cursor is normally between 0 and 100. Here, we divide this value by 100 to obtain an opacity value between 0 and 1:

```
<!DOCTYPE html>
<script src = jquery.js></script>
<script src = jqueryui/js/jquery-ui-1.8.16.custom.min.js></script>

<link rel=stylesheet type=text/css
      href=jqueryui/css/smoothness/jquery-ui-1.8.16.custom.css />

<img src=book.jpg /><br /><br />
<div id=slider></div><br />

<script>

$("div#slider").slider ({
  animate : true,
  slide : function (event)
  {
    var value = $("div#slider").slider ("value");
    var opacity = value / 100;
    $("img").css ({ opacity : opacity });
  }
```

```
	}).slider ("value", 100);

</script>
```

Figure 7-6. The opacity of the image is set at the indicated level

CHAPTER 8

Datepickers

Datepickers allow users to enter dates easily and visually, taking into account the various linguistic constraints in different countries (names of days and months, date format).

Basic Principles of Datepickers

Suppose we want to write the HTML code to display the calendar shown in Figure 8-1. This calendar appears when users click in the input field for entering a date. Months can scroll with the arrows in the top right and left of the calendar, and if you select one day it fits in the input field.

Here's how to write the HTML code according to the conventions of jQuery UI, including the `datepicker ()` method called in the `<script>` tag.

We use an `<input>` element with the date identifier, which is the entry field of the date. In this case, the calendar will automatically be positioned below the input field when a user clicks it. The calendar will be hidden when users click outside or choose a date (the date will then be displayed in the input field):

```
<script src = jquery.js></script>
<script src = jqueryui/js/jquery-ui-1.8.16.custom.min.js></script>

<link rel=stylesheet type=text/css
      href=jqueryui/css/smoothness/jquery-ui-1.8.16.custom.css />

<h3>Click to select a date :</h3>
<input id=date />

<script>

$("input#date").datepicker ();

</script>
```

Figure 8-1. A calendar in the HTML page

If we use a `<div>` or `<span>` instead of an `<input>` element, the calendar is displayed statically without users having to click in the input field to access it.

Formatting Content

The `datepicker ()` method changes the appearance of HTML elements on a page by adding new CSS classes.

Figure 8-2 shows an example of HTML generated by jQuery UI once the `datepicker ()` instruction modifies the HTML (the code was recovered using the Firebug extension in Firefox).

The input field is slightly modified by adding the `hasDatepicker` CSS class, but a `<div>` element (having the `ui-datepicker-div` CSS class) corresponding to the calendar is also inserted into the HTML. This `<div>` element will be displayed or hidden depending on whether the user wants to see the calendar or not.

```
<html>
    <head>
    <body>
        <h3>Click to select a date : </h3>
        <input id="date" class="hasDatepicker">
        <script>
        <div id="ui-datepicker-div" class="ui-datepicker ui-widget
            ui-widget-content ui-helper-clearfix ui-corner-all" style="position:
            absolute; top: 71.7167px; left: 8px; z-index: 1; display: block;">
            <div class="ui-datepicker-header ui-widget-header ui-helper-
                clearfix ui-corner-all">
                <a class="ui-datepicker-prev
                    ui-corner-all" title="Prev" onclick="DP_jQuery_1317809417530.
                    datepicker._adjustDate('#date', -1, 'M');">
                <a class="ui-datepicker-next
                    ui-corner-all" title="Next" onclick="DP_jQuery_1317809417530.
                    datepicker._adjustDate('#date', +1, 'M');">
                <div class="ui-datepicker-title">
            </div>
            <table class="ui-datepicker-calendar">
                <thead>
                <tbody>
            </table>
        </div>
    </body>
</html>
```

Figure 8-2. HTML code generated by the datepicker () method

The structure of the HTML is simple: in addition to the corresponding global <div>
calendar, it has a first <div> containing the first line of the calendar (the title for the
month and year, with two buttons for arrows for the month), then a table with the
names of the day (<thead> tag) and the corresponding days (<tbody> tag).

It is possible to use CSS classes for HTML elements to customize the display. For
example, if we change the ui-datepicker-header CSS class associated with <div> ele-
ments and the ui-datepicker-calendar class associated with <table> elements, we get
a new appearance for the calendar (see Figure 8-3). These classes are changed in the
HTML by adding a <style> tag:

```
<script src = jquery.js></script>
<script src = jqueryui/js/jquery-ui-1.8.16.custom.min.js></script>

<link rel=stylesheet type=text/css
    href=jqueryui/css/smoothness/jquery-ui-1.8.16.custom.css />

<style type=text/css>
  div.ui-datepicker-header {
    font-size : 12px;
    font-family : georgia;
  }

  table.ui-datepicker-calendar {
```

```
      font-size : 10px;
      font-family : georgia;
      font-style : italic;
    }
</style>

<h3>Click to select a date :</h3>
<input id=date />

<script>

$("input#date").datepicker ();

</script>
```

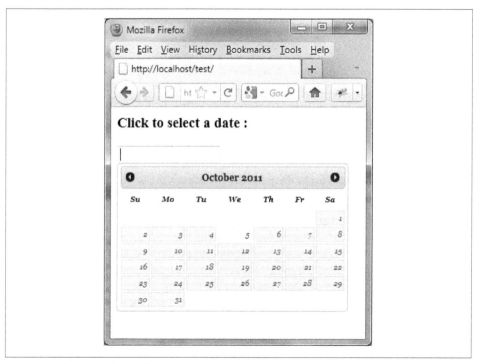

Figure 8-3. Customized calendar

The datepicker () Method

The datepicker () method can be used in two forms:

- $(selector, context).datepicker (options)
- $(selector, context).datepicker ("action", params)

The datepicker (options) Method

The `datepicker (options)` method declares that an `<input>` element (or `<div>` or `<span>`, depending on how you choose to display the calendar) should be managed as a datepicker. The `options` parameter is an object that specifies the appearance and behavior of the calendar. It can also specify the format for displaying dates in different countries.

Managing the appearance and visual effects associated with the calendar

The options listed in Table 8-1 allow us to set the appearance of the calendar.

Table 8-1. Options for managing the appearance of the calendar

Option	Function
`options.firstDay`	Integer that indicates which day begins a week on the calendar. The value 0 corresponds to Sunday (default).
`options.numberOf Months`	Number of months displayed at the same time in the calendar. For example, a value of 3 indicates the calendar will display three consecutive months.
	If it is indicated as an array, it is the number of rows and columns of months displayed. For example, [3, 2] for displaying six months, three on each line. The default is 1 (a single month).
`options.showOther Months`	If the first of the month does not fall on the day indicated in `options.firstDay`, unused cells at the beginning and end of the month can display days from the previous or following months.
	The default value is `false` (days from the preceding and following months are not shown in the unused cells of the current month).
`options.selectOther Months`	When set to `true`, indicates that the cells of the previous or next month indicated in the calendar of the current month can be selected. This option is used with `options.showO therMonths` set to `true`.
`options.changeMonth`	When set to `true`, displays a list of months for quick selection. This list appears at the top of the calendar, instead of months and the year shown. The default value is `false`.
`options.changeYear`	When set to `true`, displays a list of years for quick selection. This list appears at the top of the calendar, instead of months and the year shown. The default value is `false`.

jQuery UI can also apply appearance and disappearance effects for the calendar window, with the `options.showAnim` option. Table 8-2 describes the options, and Table 8-3 lists specific effects.

Table 8-2. Options for managing effects

Option	Function
`options.showAnim`	Name of the visual effect that will be produced during an appearance or disappearance of the calendar. By default, it is a `"fadeIn"` effect. Specify `false` to produce no effect.
`options.duration`	Duration of the appearance or disappearance effect, in milliseconds.

Table 8-3. Effects provided by jQuery and jQuery UI

Effect	Function
"fadeIn"	Make the element appear or disappear by changing its opacity.
"blind"	Make the element appear or disappear from the top.
"bounce"	Make the element appear or disappear by bouncing vertically.
"clip"	Make the element appear or disappear vertically from its center.
"drop"	Make the element appear or disappear on the left, by changing its opacity.
"fold"	Make the element appear or disappear from its upper left corner.
"highlight"	Make the element appear or disappear by changing its opacity and background color.
"puff"	Make the element appear or disappear by resizing it from its center. It appears by shrinking and disappears by growing.
"pulsate"	Make the element appear or disappear by blinking.
"scale"	Make the element appear or disappear by resizing it from its center. It disappears by shrinking and appears by growing.
"slide"	Make the element appear or disappear from the right side.

Internationalization options

By default, the calendar is displayed in English. jQuery UI can display it in most major languages (German, French, Spanish, etc.). Simply include the JavaScript file for the language. These files are located in the *jqueryui/development-bundle/ui/i18n* directory.

Once the file of the language is inserted in the HTML, some options are included by default (name of month and day, date format, etc.), but you can change them using the options listed in Table 8-4. The date format is a string specified in `options.dateFormat`, and you can configure it with the codes listed in Table 8-5.

Table 8-4. Internationalization options

Option	Function
options.dateFormat	Specifies the date format that will be retrieved from the calendar. For a date in English, the default is mm/dd/yy (according to the conventions listed in Table 8-5).
options.dayNames	Indicates an array of day names in long format (Sunday, Monday, Tuesday, etc.). The array must start on Sunday.
options.dayNamesShort	Indicates an array of day names in short format (Sun, Mon, Tue, etc.). The array must start on Sun (Sunday).
options.dayNamesMin	Indicates an array of day names in minimum size (Su, Mo, Tu, etc.). This is the name specified in the calendar for each column. The array must start on Su (Sunday).
options.monthNames	Indicates an array of month names in long format (January, February, etc.). The array should begin in January.
options.monthNamesShort	Indicates an array of month names in short format (Jan, Feb, etc.). The array must begin in Jan (January).

Table 8-5. Date formatting codes

Code	Function
d	Day of the month, from 1 to 31.
dd	Day of the month, from 01 to 31.
o	Day of the year, from 1 to 366.
oo	Day of the year, from 001 to 366.
D	Day's name, in short form (Mon, Tue, etc.).
DD	Day's name, in long form (Monday, Tuesday, etc.).
m	Month from 1 to 12.
mm	Month from 01 to 12.
M	Month's name, in short form (Jan, Feb, etc.).
MM	The name of the month in long form (January, February, etc.).
y	Year as two digits (12 for 2012).
yy	Year as four digits (2012).
@	Number of milliseconds since the 01/01/1970.

You can combine these codes to form complete dates according to your preferred order (e.g., the day before or after the month). You can insert additional characters, such as slash (/) or the hyphen (-), to separate fields.

Managing date selection

By default, all calendar dates can be selected, including the month following or preceding the current month. It is possible to limit this choice by specifying a minimum or maximum date. Table 8-6 lists options for date selection.

Table 8-6. Options for managing date selection

Option	Function
`options.minDate`	Minimum selectable date in the calendar.
`options.maxDate`	Maximum selectable date in the calendar.
`options.defaultDate`	Preset default date when no date has been previously selected. This date will be displayed in the first display of the calendar. By default, this is the current date.

The values of these options are dates that can be expressed either as a Date object (created by new Date ()), the number of days before (e.g., –2) or after (e.g., 2) the current date, or by a string taking one of the forms presented in Table 8-7.

Table 8-7. Forms of the string representing the date to select

Format	Function	Example
X	X days after the current date (where X ranges from 1 to n).	1, 2, 3
-X	X days before the current date (where X ranges from 1 to n)	−1, −2, −3
Xm	X months after the current date (where X ranges from 1 to n)	1m, 2m, 3m
-Xm	X months before the current date (where X ranges from 1 to n)	−1m, −2m, −3m
Xw	X weeks after the current date (where X ranges from 1 to n)	1w, 2w, 3w
-Xw	X weeks before the current date (where X ranges from 1 to n)	−1w, −2w, −3w

Any combination of days, weeks, and months can produce a day in relation to the current date. For example, 1m+3,-1m-1w.

Managing events on the calendar

Table 8-8 lists options you can use to manage the events on the calendar

Table 8-8. Options for managing events on the calendar

Option	Function
options.beforeShow	The beforeShow () method is called before the calendar is displayed.
options.beforeShowDay	The beforeShowDay (date) method is called for each day (corresponding to the date parameter, which is an object of Date class) displayed in the calendar. The method must return an array to indicate the following for each date: • Whether it is selectable (true in [0]) • CSS classes used in this calendar's cell (in [1], "" by default) • A string displayed as a tooltip on the cell (in [2], "" by default).
options.onChangeMonth Year	The onChangeMonthYear (year, month) method is called when the month or year displayed in the calendar changes. This occurs when the user clicks the buttons at the top of the calendar or when options.changeMonth or options.changeYear is set to true while the user selects another month or another year from the list.
options.onClose	The onClose (dateText) method is called when the calendar is closed (by selecting a date, clicking outside the calendar, or pressing Esc). The dateText parameter is the date as text (in the format corresponding to options.dateFormat) to be written into the input field.
options.onSelect	The onSelect (dateText) method is called when a date was selected in the calendar. The dateText parameter is the date as text (in the format corresponding to options.dateFormat) to be written into the input field.

jQuery UI allows the use of only the event methods defined by the previous options (options.beforeShow, etc.). The use of the bind () method to manage calendars is not allowed for now.

The datepicker ("action", params) Method

The datepicker ("action", params) method can perform an action on the calendar, such as selecting a new date. The action is specified as a string in the first argument (e.g., "show" to display the calendar). The available actions are listed in Table 8-9.

Table 8-9. The datepicker ("action", params) method actions

Action	Function
datepicker ("show")	Show calendar.
datepicker ("hide")	Hide calendar.
datepicker ("get Date")	Return a Date object corresponding to the selected date.
	If the date format is not specified (options.dateFormat), the date is presented in the form mm/dd/yy, even if the JavaScript file for the country is included. Make sure to always specify options.dateFormat if you use datepicker ("getDate") with a format other than English.
datepicker ("set Date", date)	Initialize a preset date in the calendar. The date parameter is expressed as noted above (Date object, number of days before or after the current date, or string).
	If the date format is not specified (options.dateFormat), the date is presented in the form mm/dd/yy, even if the JavaScript file for the country is included. Make sure to always specify options.dateFormat if you use datepicker ("setDate") with a format other than English.
datepicker ("option", param)	Retrieve the value of the param option specified. This option corresponds to one of those used with datepicker (options).
datepicker ("option", param, value)	Change the value of the param option. This option corresponds to one of those used with datepicker (options).
datepicker ("destroy")	Remove the management of calendars. Calendars revert to simple HTML without CSS class or event management.

Examples of Using Datepickers

This section includes some practical examples of using datepickers.

Displaying a Calendar in Another Language

To display a calendar in another language (as shown in Figure 8-4), simply include the JavaScript file associated with that language. This file is located in the *jqueryui/development-bundle/ui/i18n* directory, such as the *jqueryui/development-bundle/ui/i18n/jquery.ui.datepicker-fr.js* file for the French language:

```
<script src = jquery.js></script>
<script src = jqueryui/js/jquery-ui-1.8.16.custom.min.js></script>
<script src=jqueryui/development-bundle/ui/i18n/jquery.ui.datepicker-fr.js></script>

<link rel=stylesheet type=text/css
      href=jqueryui/css/smoothness/jquery-ui-1.8.16.custom.css />

<h3>Click to select a date :</h3>
<input id=date />

<script>

$("input#date").datepicker ();

</script>
```

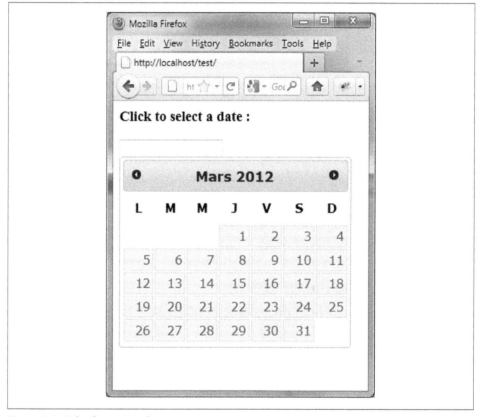

Figure 8-4. Calendar in French

Displaying Multiple Months in the Calendar

Several months can be displayed in the calendar (Figure 8-5). For this, we use `options.numberOfMonths`, which indicates the desired number of months or an array [x, y] that contains the number of rows (x) and columns (y) that represent these months.

Use the following (in bold) to display a calendar of four months (two rows of two, shown in Figure 8-5):

```
<script src=jquery.js></script>
<script src=jqueryui/development-bundle/ui/jquery-ui-1.8.4.custom.js></script>
<script src=jqueryui/development-bundle/ui/i18n/jquery.ui.datepicker-fr.js>
</script>

<link rel=stylesheet type=text/css
    href="jqueryui/development-bundle/themes/smoothness/jquery.ui.all.css" />

<body>
<input id=date />
</body>

<script>

$("input#date").datepicker ({
  numberOfMonths : [2, 2]
});

</script>
```

In this example, we see that the cells preceding the first day of the month and those after the last day of the month are empty. We can ensure that the days of the previous month and those of the next month are inserted in these cells to make the calendar more harmonious, as shown in Figure 8-6. This is done using the `options.showOtherMonths` option set to `true`:

```
<script src = jquery.js></script>
<script src = jqueryui/js/jquery-ui-1.8.16.custom.min.js></script>

<link rel=stylesheet type=text/css
    href=jqueryui/css/smoothness/jquery-ui-1.8.16.custom.css />

<h3>Click to select a date :</h3>
<input id=date />

<script>

$("input#date").datepicker ({
  numberOfMonths : [2, 2],
  showOtherMonths : true
});

</script>
```

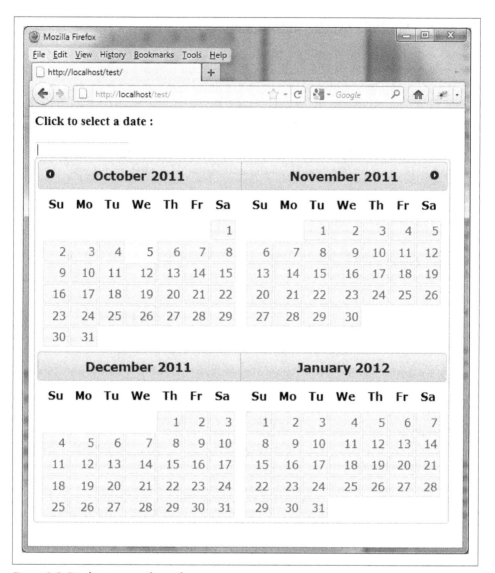

Figure 8-5. Displaying several months

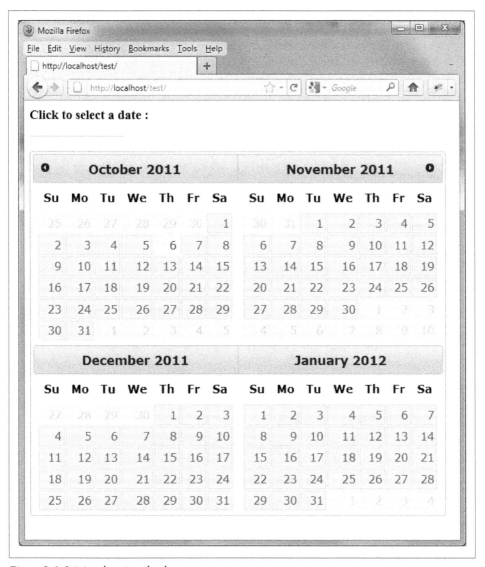

Figure 8-6. Joining days in calendars

Displaying a Static Calendar

It is possible to display a calendar that is directly in the HTML page instead of being displayed only when users click in the input field associated with it (Figure 8-7). For this, we replace the input field with a <span> or <div> element:

```
<script src = jquery.js></script>
<script src = jqueryui/js/jquery-ui-1.8.16.custom.min.js></script>

<link rel=stylesheet type=text/css
      href=jqueryui/css/smoothness/jquery-ui-1.8.16.custom.css />

<div> Before the calendar </div>
<div id=date></div>
<div> After the calendar </div>

<script>

$("div#date").datepicker ();

</script>
```

Figure 8-7. Static calendar

Indicating Minimum and Maximum Dates

The `options.minDate` and `options.maxDate` options can indicate a minimum and maximum date (Figure 8-8). For example, to prevent the selection of a date earlier than three days before the current date or later than a week after the current date, we write the following:

```
<script src = jquery.js></script>
<script src = jqueryui/js/jquery-ui-1.8.16.custom.min.js></script>

<link rel=stylesheet type=text/css
      href=jqueryui/css/smoothness/jquery-ui-1.8.16.custom.css />

<h3>Click to select a date :</h3>
<input id=date />

<script>

$("input#date").datepicker ({
  minDate : -3,           // at least three days before the current date
  maxDate : "1w"          // maximum one week after the current date
});

</script>
```

Figure 8-8. Minimum and maximum dates

Suppose the current date is October 6, 2011. Around it, the selectable days are shown on a gray background with a darker color, while the days that cannot be selected are displayed in a lighter gray and do not respond to mouse events.

Preventing the Selection of Specific Dates

The `options.minDate` and `options.maxDate` options can indicate a range of selectable dates, but do not allow us to define multiple non-concurrent dates. For example, for a firm open Monday to Friday, it is not possible with these options to prevent selection of any Saturdays and Sundays (Figure 8-9).

The `options.beforeShowDay` option is a method called for each day displayed on the calendar. For each day, it is shown in the returned array as selected or not.

The `beforeShowDay (date)` method must return an array whose first element (index 0) contains `true` (the date is selected) or `false` (not selected):

```
<script src = jquery.js></script>
<script src = jqueryui/js/jquery-ui-1.8.16.custom.min.js></script>

<link rel=stylesheet type=text/css
      href=jqueryui/css/smoothness/jquery-ui-1.8.16.custom.css />

<h3>Click to select a date :</h3>
<input id=date />

<script>

$("input#date").datepicker ({
  beforeShowDay : function (date)
  {
    var dayOfWeek = date.getDay ();    // 0 : Sunday, 1 : Monday, ...
    if (dayOfWeek == 0 || dayOfWeek == 6) return [false];
    else return [true];
  }
});

</script>
```

Preselecting Any Date

The preset default date is the current date. To preselect a different date, use the `options.defaultDate` option or `datepicker ("setDate", date)` method.

Using options.defaultDate

While the current date corresponds to October 6, we want to preselect the date corresponding to October 28 (Figure 8-10).

Figure 8-9. Saturdays and Sundays are no longer available for selection

```
<script src = jquery.js></script>
<script src = jqueryui/js/jquery-ui-1.8.16.custom.min.js></script>

<link rel=stylesheet type=text/css
      href=jqueryui/css/smoothness/jquery-ui-1.8.16.custom.css />

<h3>Click to select a date :</h3>
<input id=date />

<script>

$("input#date").datepicker ({
  defaultDate : "3w+1"
});

</script>
```

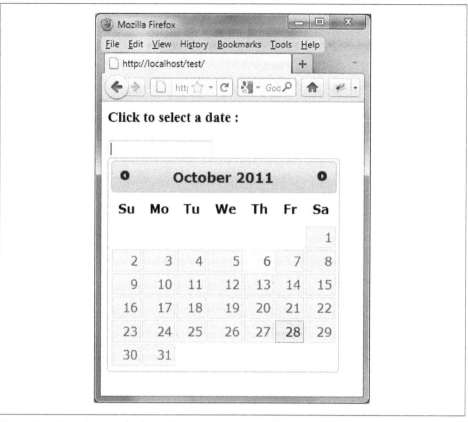

Figure 8-10. Preselection of a date other than the current date

Using datepicker ("setDate", date)

The preselection of a date can also be done using the `datepicker ("setDate", date)` method. As before, preselect a date three weeks and a day later than the current date:

```
<script src = jquery.js></script>
<script src = jqueryui/js/jquery-ui-1.8.16.custom.min.js></script>

<link rel=stylesheet type=text/css
     href=jqueryui/css/smoothness/jquery-ui-1.8.16.custom.css />

<h3>Click to select a date :</h3>
<input id=date />

<script>

$("input#date").datepicker ().datepicker ("setDate", "3w+1");

</script>
```

With this second method, the difference from the previous is that the date input field is initialized with the specified date (Figure 8-11).

Figure 8-11. The preselected date appears in the input field

Special case of dates in foreign formats

If you use a calendar in a foreign language, it must also indicate the date format in the country selected by the `options.dateFormat` option. The default format is `"mm/dd/yy"` corresponding to the calendar in English. To preset a date in a calendar in French, for example, we write the following:

```
<script src = jquery.js></script>
<script src = jqueryui/js/jquery-ui-1.8.16.custom.min.js></script>
<script src=jqueryui/development-bundle/ui/i18n/jquery.ui.datepicker-fr.js></script>

<link rel=stylesheet type=text/css
      href=jqueryui/css/smoothness/jquery-ui-1.8.16.custom.css />

<h3>Click to select a date :</h3>
<input id=date />
```

```
<script>

$("input#date").datepicker ({
  dateFormat : "dd/mm/yy"            // required to use setDate
}).datepicker ("setDate", "3w+1");

</script>
```

The result is shown in Figure 8-12.

Figure 8-12. A preselected date in a French calendar

Performing an Ajax Request When Selecting a Date

It is common to perform an Ajax request for date selection. In this example, we choose a date from the calendar and transmit it to the server, which returns the date back to us. This validates the full path of information transmission:

```
<script src = jquery.js></script>
<script src = jqueryui/js/jquery-ui-1.8.16.custom.min.js></script>

<link rel=stylesheet type=text/css
      href=jqueryui/css/smoothness/jquery-ui-1.8.16.custom.css />

<h3>Click to select a date :</h3>
<input id=date />
<div id=datereturn></div>

<script>

$("input#date").datepicker ({
  onSelect : function (dateText)
  {
    var data = { date : dateText };
    $.ajax ({
    url : "action.php",
    data : data,
    complete : function (xhr, result)
    {
      if (result != "success") return;
      var response = xhr.responseText;
      $("#datereturn").html (response);
    }
  });
  }
});

</script>
```

The text returned by the server will be inserted into the <div> element with the datereturn identifier. The code on the server is shown in the *action.php* file below:

```
<?
  $date = $_REQUEST["date"];

  $txt = "Selected date: <i> $date </i>";
  $txt = utf8_encode($txt);
  echo ($txt);
?>
```

Notice that the URL *http://localhost/test* is an HTTP URL. If it is not, the Ajax call will not work.

After being selected, the date appears below the input field (Figure 8-13).

Figure 8-13. The selected date is transmitted to the server

Autocompletion

Autocompletion is a mechanism frequently used in modern websites to provide the user with a list of suggestions for the beginning of the word he has typed in a text box. He can then select an item from the list, which will be displayed in the input field. This feature prevents the user from having to enter an entire word or a set of words.

Basic Principles of Autocompletion

Suppose we want to write the HTML code to display the list of suggestions shown in Figure 9-1, which appears when users type the letter "p." This displays a list in which each element contains at least one letter "p."

The input field is represented by an `<input>` whose ID is `book`:

```
<script src = jquery.js></script>
<script src = jqueryui/js/jquery-ui-1.8.16.custom.min.js></script>

<link rel=stylesheet type=text/css
      href=jqueryui/css/smoothness/jquery-ui-1.8.16.custom.css />

<h3>Enter the name of the book:</h3>
<input id=book />

<script>

// array of items to be proposed in the list of suggestions
var books = ["Web development with J2EE", "Practical CSS & JavaScript",
             "Practical Ruby on Rails", "Introduction to HTML & CSS",
             "jQuery UI"];

$("input#book").autocomplete ({
  source : books
});

</script>
```

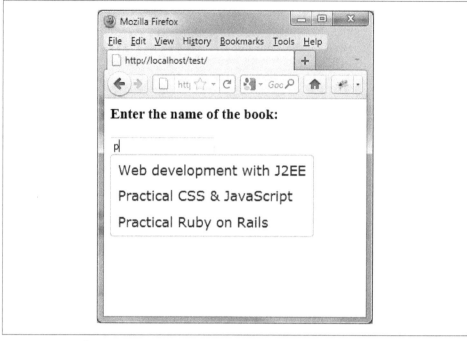

Figure 9-1. List of suggestions

In the `<script>` tag of the HTML page, we need to indicate both the list of suggestions (`var books`) and that the input field must be observed in order to display the list of suggestions. To do this, simply indicate that the `<input>` field is managed by the jQuery UI `autocomplete ()` method. The `{source: books}` specifies options needed to display the list of suggestions.

Formatting Content

The `autocomplete ()` method creates a list of suggestions below the input field and adds new CSS classes to the elements concerned to give them the appropriate style.

In Figure 9-2, for example, the HTML generated by jQuery UI is modified by the `autocomplete ()` instruction (the code was recovered using the Firebug extension in Firefox).

The `<input>` element is slightly modified, while the HTML now contains a `<ul>` corresponding to the list that appears below the input field. Each element of the list is a `<li>` with a `ui-menu-item` CSS class.

We can customize the display by editing the CSS classes with the addition of a `<style>` tag. For example, if we modify the `ui-menu-item` class associated with `<li>` elements, we can change the font used for the list of suggestions, as shown in Figure 9-3:

```
<script src = jquery.js></script>
<script src = jqueryui/js/jquery-ui-1.8.16.custom.min.js></script>

<link rel=stylesheet type=text/css
      href=jqueryui/css/smoothness/jquery-ui-1.8.16.custom.css />

<style type=text/css>
  li.ui-menu-item {
    font-size : 12px;
    font-family : georgia;
  }
</style>

<h3>Enter the name of the book:</h3>
<input id=book />

<script>

// array of items to be proposed in the list of suggestions
var books = ["Web development with J2EE", "Practical CSS & JavaScript",
             "Practical Ruby on Rails", "Introduction to HTML & CSS",
             "jQuery UI"];

$("input#book").autocomplete ({
  source : books
});

</script>
```

Figure 9-2. HTML code generated by the autocomplete () method

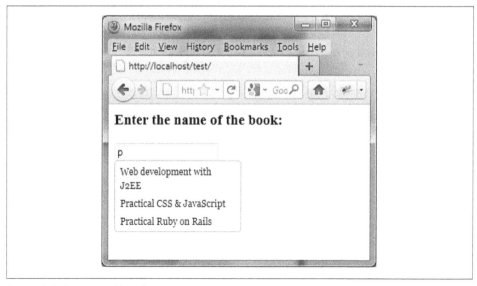

Figure 9-3. Customized list of suggestions

The autocomplete () Method

The autocomplete () method can be used in two forms:

- $(selector, context).autocomplete (options)
- $(selector, context).autocomplete ("action", params)

The autocomplete (options) Method

The autocomplete (options) method declares that an <input> HTML element must be managed as an input field that will be displayed above a list of suggestions. The options parameter specifies the behavior of the list of suggestions when the user is typing in the input field.

The operation of autocompletion is as follows: from the characters introduced in the input field, a match is made in the specified source (in options.source). Matching can be done with any character from the source, not just the beginning of it. Thus, if one looks for the letter "a," it does not have to be located at the beginning of words, but can be located in the middle.

Managing autocompletion

Table 9-1 details the options that are available for managing autocompletion.

Table 9-1. Options for managing autocompletion

Option	Function
options.disabled	When set to `true`, disables the autocompletion mechanism. Users can enter characters into the text field, but no list appears. Use `autocomplete ("enable")` to enable the autocompletion mechanism.
options.source	Indicates the data source to use for the list of suggestions. Data can be local (already known in the program) or remote (retrieved from the server).
options.minLength	Minimum number of characters to enter in the field to start the display of the list of suggestions. By default, this number is 1.
options.delay	Timeout (in milliseconds) before the entered characters are taken into account. By default, this delay is 300 ms.

Managing events in the list of suggestions

The events described in Table 9-2 are generated either by typing in the input field, by selecting an item in the list, or by calling one of the methods for the autocompletion management. In each of these methods, the `<ul>` containing the list is accessible via `autocomplete ("widget")`. This is useful when you want to manipulate the list in its entirety, then eventually to access to each `<li>` list item.

Table 9-2. Options for managing autocompletion events

Option	Function
options.open	The `open (event)` method is called when the list of suggestions will be displayed.
options.close	The `close (event)` method is called when the list of suggestions will be closed.
options.search	The `search (event)` method is called when a search should be done to display the corresponding list of suggestions. If the method returns `false`, the list is not displayed.
options.focus	The `focus (event, ui)` method is called when a list item has the focus, either from a mouseover or by selection with the arrow keys.
	The `ui.item` value is a `{label, value}` object corresponding to the label text displayed in the list of suggestions, while `value` is the value that will be inserted into the input field if the list item is selected (`label` and `value` often have the same value, but this distinction allows more flexibility).
options.select	The `select (event, ui)` method is called when a list item is selected.
	The `ui.item` value is a `{label, value}` object corresponding to the label text displayed in the list of suggestions, while `value` is the value that will be inserted into the input field if the list item is selected (`label` and `value` often have the same value, but this distinction allows more flexibility).
	If the method returns `false`, the contents of the input field are not changed.
options.change	The `change (event)` method is called when the input field loses focus (when the user clicks outside of it), while the field content has changed. This can occur if the user selects a new item in the list then enters new text in the field and leaves it.

The autocomplete ("action", params) Method

The autocomplete ("action", params) method can perform an action on the list of suggestions, such as show or hide. The action is specified as a string in the first argument (e.g., "close" to hide the list). These actions are listed in Table 9-3.

Table 9-3. The autocomplete ("action", params) method actions

Action	Function
autocomplete ("disable")	Disable the autocompletion mechanism. The list of suggestions no longer appears.
autocomplete ("enable")	Reactivate the autocompletion mechanism. The list of suggestions will again be displayed.
autocomplete ("search", value)	Search for correspondence between the string value and the data source (specified in options.source). The minimum number of characters (indicated in options.minLength) must be reached in value, otherwise the search is not performed.
	Once a list of suggestions is found, it appears under the corresponding item.
autocomplete ("close")	Hide the list of suggestions.
autocomplete ("widget")	Retrieve the <ul> DOM element corresponding to the list of suggestions. This is an object of jQuery class that allows easy access to the list without using jQuery selectors.
autocomplete ("option", param)	Retrieve the value of the specified param option. This option corresponds to one of those used with autocomplete (options).
autocomplete ("option", param, value)	Change the value of the param option. This option corresponds to one of those used with autocomplete (options).
autocomplete ("destroy")	Remove autocompletion management. Lists of suggestions are deleted.

Event Management on the List of Suggestions with bind ()

In addition to the event methods provided in the options of the autocomplete (options) method, jQuery UI allows us to manage these events using the bind () method (detailed in Table 9-4).

Table 9-4. Events created by jQuery UI

Event	Function
autocompleteopen	Same meaning as options.open.
autocompleteclose	Same meaning as options.close.
autocompletesearch	Same meaning as options.search.
autocompletefocus	Same meaning as options.focus.
autocompleteselect	Same meaning as options.select.
autocompletechange	Same meaning as options.change.

Examples of Using the Autocompletion Mechanism

Now that you understand how to use and manage suggestion lists, let's create some scripts that implement the autocompletion mechanism.

Specifying the Width of the List of Suggestions

jQuery UI itself calculates the width of the list of suggestions based on its content. However, it may be useful to specify the width of the list manually. In this example, we set the list of suggestions to 400 pixels wide (see Figure 9-4):

```
<script src = jquery.js></script>
<script src = jqueryui/js/jquery-ui-1.8.16.custom.min.js></script>

<link rel=stylesheet type=text/css
      href=jqueryui/css/smoothness/jquery-ui-1.8.16.custom.css />

<h3>Enter the name of the book:</h3>
<input id=book />

<script>

// array of items to be proposed in the list of suggestions
var books = ["Web development with J2EE", "Practical CSS & JavaScript",
             "Practical Ruby on Rails", "Introduction to HTML & CSS",
             "jQuery UI"];

$("input#book").autocomplete ({
  source : books,
  open : function (event)
  {
    var $ul = $(this).autocomplete ("widget");
    $ul.css ("width", "400px");
  }
});

</script>
```

The list corresponds to the <ul> (created automatically by jQuery UI when using the autocomplete (options) method). It was explained earlier that it was easier to retrieve it using the autocomplete ("widget") instruction.

Once this <ul> element is recovered (through its jQuery class object), simply resize it using the css () instruction. This can be done only when the list will be displayed, hence the use of the options.open option.

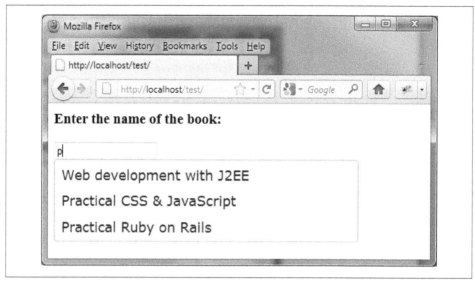

Figure 9-4. Manual width setting for a list of suggestions

Displaying a List of Suggestions at the Opening of the HTML Page

The list of suggestions will appear as soon as the required number of characters is entered in the input field (this number is indicated in `options.minLength`). This means having to type at least one character (a value of 0 in `options.minLength` is not enough to cause the immediate display of the list of suggestions).

Let's create an example that shows a list of suggestions as soon as the script runs (users are not required to enter any characters in the input field). To do this, use the `autocomplete ("search", "")` method at the start of the script. The required number of characters here is 0 (specified by the empty string, `""`). The list will be displayed with all possible values and won't permit entries in the text field (Figure 9-5):

```
<script src = jquery.js></script>
<script src = jqueryui/js/jquery-ui-1.8.16.custom.min.js></script>

<link rel=stylesheet type=text/css
    href=jqueryui/css/smoothness/jquery-ui-1.8.16.custom.css />

<h3>Enter the name of the book:</h3>
<input id=book />

<script>

// array of items to be proposed in the list of suggestions
var books = ["Web development with J2EE", "Practical CSS & JavaScript",
            "Practical Ruby on Rails", "Introduction to HTML & CSS",
            "jQuery UI"];
```

```
$("input#book").autocomplete ({
   source : books,
   minLength : 0
}).autocomplete ("search", "");
```

```
</script>
```

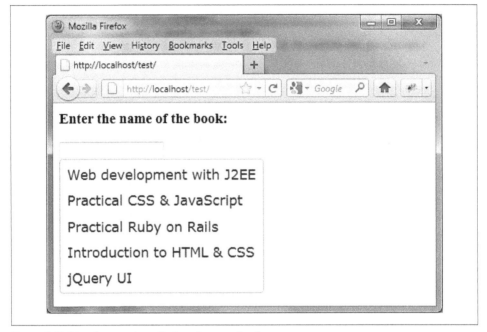

Figure 9-5. List of suggestions displayed at page load

Rather than showing a list of suggestions when the page is opened, we can show the list when the user clicks in the input field, as explained in the following example.

Displaying a List of Suggestions at the Entry of the Cursor in the Input Field

This is a variant of previous script. When the user clicks in the input field, the list is displayed immediately. The search for list items to display is this time related to the focus event on the input field:

```
<script src = jquery.js></script>
<script src = jqueryui/js/jquery-ui-1.8.16.custom.min.js></script>

<link rel=stylesheet type=text/css
      href=jqueryui/css/smoothness/jquery-ui-1.8.16.custom.css />

<h3>Enter the name of the book:</h3>
<input id=book />

<script>
```

```
// array of items to be proposed in the list of suggestions
var books = ["Web development with J2EE", "Practical CSS & JavaScript",
             "Practical Ruby on Rails", "Introduction to HTML & CSS",
             "jQuery UI"];

$("input#book").autocomplete ({
  source : books,
  minLength : 0
}).focus (function (event)
{
  $(this).autocomplete ("search", "");
});

</script>
```

Producing an Effect on the Appearance of the List of Suggestions

By default, the list is displayed as soon as it is returned by jQuery UI. It is possible to produce an effect before it is displayed, such as a slideDown effect:

```
<script src = jquery.js></script>
<script src = jqueryui/js/jquery-ui-1.8.16.custom.min.js></script>

<link rel=stylesheet type=text/css
      href=jqueryui/css/smoothness/jquery-ui-1.8.16.custom.css />

<h3>Enter the name of the book:</h3>
<input id=book />

<script>

// array of items to be proposed in the list of suggestions
var books = ["Web development with J2EE", "Practical CSS & JavaScript",
             "Practical Ruby on Rails", "Introduction to HTML & CSS",
             "jQuery UI"];

$("input#book").autocomplete ({
  source : books,
  open : function (event)
  {
    var $ul = $(this).autocomplete ("widget");
    $ul.hide ().slideDown (600);
  }
});

</script>
```

Here, we use the open option, which corresponds to an event called just before the display of the list. Before this, we hide this list with hide () so it can be displayed by the slideDown effect.

If you use a hide effect, these effects are more complex to implement, due to the up-dating of the input field. Although the effect occurs, it inhibits updating in the input field with the value of the selected list item.

Dynamically Creating a List of Suggestions

The above examples all use a fixed list of suggestions, known at the start of the script. jQuery UI allows us to specify in `options.source` a source of data as a callback function that will be used to build the list of suggestions:

```
<script src = jquery.js></script>
<script src = jqueryui/js/jquery-ui-1.8.16.custom.min.js></script>

<link rel=stylesheet type=text/css
        href=jqueryui/css/smoothness/jquery-ui-1.8.16.custom.css />

<h3>Enter the name of the book:</h3>
<input id=book />

<script>

$("input#book").autocomplete ({
  source : function (request, callback)
  {
    // array of items to be proposed in the list of suggestions
    var books = ["Web development with J2EE", "Practical CSS & JavaScript",
                 "Practical Ruby on Rails", "Introduction to HTML & CSS",
                 "jQuery UI"];

    callback (books);
  }
a});

</script>
```

In `options.source`, we indicate a function used to build the list of suggestions. This function takes two parameters:

- `request` is an object having the `term` property indicating the text entered in the input field (property not used here).
- `callback` is a function that must be called at the end of treatment, indicating as a parameter the list of suggestions (`books` here), in array form.

In this example, the text typed by the user is not used, so the returned list is always the same, regardless of the value entered by the user (Figure 9-6). We will see in the fol-lowing section how to consider the characters entered in the input field.

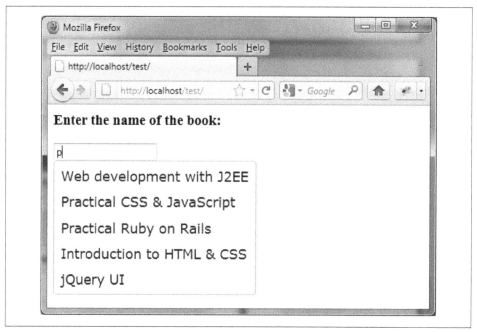

Figure 9-6. List of suggestions created dynamically

Dynamically Creating a List of Suggestions Based on the Input Data

We can improve the previous program by taking the input and making an Ajax call to the server, to retrieve a list of suggestions to display.

The books are stored in a MySQL database (here the test database containing the books table). Its description and its contents are as follows:

```
CREATE DATABASE IF NOT EXISTS test;
USE test;
DROP TABLE IF EXISTS books;
CREATE TABLE books (
  id int(10) unsigned NOT NULL auto_increment,
  title varchar(100) NOT NULL,
  PRIMARY KEY  (id)
);

INSERT INTO books (id, title) VALUES
  (1,"Web development with J2EE"),
  (2,"Practical CSS & JavaScript"),
  (3,"Practical Ruby on Rails"),
  (4,"Introduction to HTML & CSS"),
  (5,"jQuery UI");

Perform an ajax call that returns the list of suggestions to display
```

```
<script src = jquery.js></script>
<script src = jqueryui/js/jquery-ui-1.8.16.custom.min.js></script>

<link rel=stylesheet type=text/css
      href=jqueryui/css/smoothness/jquery-ui-1.8.16.custom.css />

<h3>Enter the name of the book:</h3>
<input id=book />

<script>

$("input#book").autocomplete ({
  source : function (request, callback)
  {
    var data = { term : request.term };
    $.ajax ({
      url : "action.php",
      data : data,
      complete : function (xhr, result)
      {
        if (result != "success") return;
        var response = xhr.responseText;
        var books = [];

        $(response).filter ("li").each (function ()
        {
          books.push ($(this).text ());
        });
        callback (books);
      }
    });
  }
});

</script>
```

Text entered by the user is retrieved in `request.term`. An Ajax call is then made. At its completion, the server response is analyzed: it retrieves the contents of each `<li>` element, which we put in a books array, and it is then returned by `callback (books)` to be displayed.

The server program processing the Ajax request is shown in the following *action.php* file:

```
<?
  $term = $_REQUEST["term"];
  $term = utf8_decode ($term);

  $bd = mysql_connect ("localhost", "root", "pwd");
  $ret = mysql_select_db ("test", $bd);
  $query = sprintf (
        "SELECT * FROM books WHERE title LIKE '%%%s%%'",
        mysql_real_escape_string($term));

  // Query execution
```

```
    $result = mysql_query($query);
    if ($result)
    {
      // Use the result (sent to the browser)
      while ($row = mysql_fetch_assoc($result))
      {
        echo ("<li>" . utf8_encode ($row["title"]) . "</li>");
      }
      mysql_free_result($result);
    }

    mysql_close ($bd);
?>
```

This example displays the list of suggestions as text. It is also possible to insert images in list items, such as images associated with each book. This is discussed in the following section.

Inserting Images in the List of Suggestions

Autocompletion functionality provided by jQuery UI does not, as standard, insert anything other than text. You can insert other HTML elements in the list, with some manipulation of the DOM tree.

To explain this, let's take the book example. We now want to add a picture in front of each book title. If no image is available for a book, a default image is displayed instead (Figure 9-7).

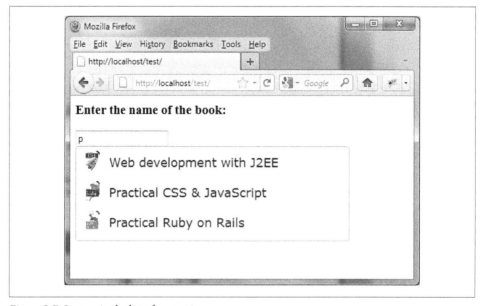

Figure 9-7. Images in the list of suggestions

To do this, you can start again with the written programs above. The database is modified to take account of the picture field containing the image filename associated with each book. This field will be set to NULL in the database if you have to display the default image:

```
CREATE DATABASE IF NOT EXISTS test;
USE test;
DROP TABLE IF EXISTS books;
CREATE TABLE books (
  id int(10) unsigned NOT NULL auto_increment,
  title varchar(100) NOT NULL,
  picture varchar(100),
  PRIMARY KEY  (id)
);

INSERT INTO books (id, title, picture) VALUES
  (1,"Web development with J2EE", "j2ee.jpg"),
  (2,"Practical CSS & JavaScript", "javascript.jpg"),
  (3,"Practical Ruby on Rails", "rails.jpg"),
  (4,"Introduction to HTML & CSS", "html.jpg"),
  (5,"jQuery UI", NULL);
```

The jQuery UI book does not have an associated image, so it uses the insertion of a null value for the picture field. Each image file (*j2ee.jpg, javascript.jpg,* etc.) will be inserted into an *images* directory on the server.

The program on the server becomes the following *action.php* file:

```
<?
  $term = $_REQUEST["term"];
  $term = utf8_decode ($term);

  $bd = mysql_connect ("localhost", "root",
"pwd");
  $ret = mysql_select_db ("test", $bd);
  $query = sprintf (
          "SELECT * FROM books WHERE title LIKE '%%%s%%'",
          mysql_real_escape_string($term));

  // Query execution
  $result = mysql_query($query);
  if ($result)
  {
    // Use the result (sent to the browser)
    header ("content-type:text/xml");    // sending XML!
    echo ("<books>");
    while ($row = mysql_fetch_assoc($result))
    {
      echo ("<li>");
      echo ("<title>"
          .
utf8_encode (str_replace ("&", "&amp;", $row["title"]))
          .
"</title>");
      echo ("<picture>" . utf8_encode
```

```
    ($row["picture"]) . "</picture>");
        echo ("</li>");
      }
      echo ("</books>");
      mysql_free_result($result);
    }

  mysql_close ($bd);
?>
```

Compared with the previous program, the change is in the format of data returned. Indeed, we must now return the book title and name of the image file. For this, we use `<title>` and `<picture>` tags grouped in a `<li>` tag. Since we use non-HTML tag names (as `<picture>`), it is necessary to indicate that the server returns XML, hence the header ("content-type:text/xml") statement.

In addition, the titles of the books may contain special XML characters such as &. This character must be converted to &amp so that the JavaScript program can correctly interpret the result given by the server.

The program of the HTML page is as follows:

```
<script src = jquery.js></script>
<script src = jqueryui/js/jquery-ui-1.8.16.custom.min.js></script>

<link rel=stylesheet type=text/css
      href=jqueryui/css/smoothness/jquery-ui-1.8.16.custom.css />

<h3>Enter the name of the book:</h3>
<input id=book />

<script>

$("input#book").autocomplete ({
  source : function (request, callback)
  {
    var data = { term : request.term };
    $.ajax ({
      url : "action.php",
      data : data,
      complete : function (xhr, result)
      {
        if (result != "success") return;
        var response = xhr.responseXML;
        var books = [];

        // recovery of titles
        $(response).find ("li title").each (function ()
        {
          books.push ($(this).text ());
        });

        // insertion of titles
        callback (books);
```

```
    // insertion of images
    var $ul = $("input#book").autocomplete ("widget");
    $(response).find ("li picture").each (function (index)
    {
      var src = $(this).text () || "default.jpg";
      $ul.find ("li:eq(" + index +") a")
          .wrapInner ("<span style=position:relative;" +
                      "top:-7px;left:10px></span>")
          .prepend ("<img src=images/" + src + " height=30 />");
    });
    }
  });
  },
  open : function (event)
  {
    var $ul = $(this).autocomplete ("widget");
    $ul.css ("width", "400px");
  }
});

</script>
```

The principle is as follows: first we build the list with the titles (thanks to the `callback (books)` instruction), then we modify the DOM tree by inserting a picture in front of each label title.

For this, the book titles are retrieved by `$(response).find ("li title")`, while the URL of the image files are collected by `$(response).find ("li picture")`. For each image (if an image does not exist, it is replaced by *default.jpg*), we get the `<a>` link previously built by the `callback (books)` instruction. It is sufficient for that link to surround the link text by a `<span>` element (using `wrapInner ()`) then insert the image at the beginning of the link (`prepend ()` instruction).

Drag-and-Drop

Drag-and-drop is a common operation in web pages for moving an item (using the mouse to drop the item on another page element). For example, if the page displays images of articles to be purchased, users can drag an item into a cart that symbolizes all the goods to be purchased.

jQuery UI can manage these operations, distinguishing the operation of "drag" (the movement of an object) and the operation of "drop" (the depositing of the item being moved). For this, jQuery UI offers both the draggable () and droppable () methods.

The draggable () Method

The draggable () method manages elements of the HTML page you want to move. This method can be used in two forms:

- $(selector, context).draggable (options)
- $(selector, context).draggable ("action", params)

The draggable (options) Method

The draggable (options) method declares that an HTML element can be moved in the HTML page. The options parameter is an object that specifies the behavior of the elements involved.

Specifying the movable elements

Use the options in Table 10-1 to indicate which elements can be moved. By default, these are all elements of the list on which the draggable (options) method applies. These options can inhibit the displacement for all items or only some, or even for moving a new item created on the fly.

Table 10-1. Options for managing movable elements

Option	Function
options.disabled	When set to true, disables the ability to move items. Items cannot be moved until this function is enabled (using the draggable ("enable") instruction).
options.cancel	Indicates a selector representing elements for which the move is prohibited. This allows you to restrict the starting list (those on which the draggable (options) method applies).
options.helper	Creates and moves a copy of the selected item.
	The "clone" value indicates that the item is duplicated and that it is the new element that moves, while the original remains in its original position.
	With "original" (the default), the initial element is moved.
	If you specify a callback function, it creates and returns a new element that will be moved. In any case, if a new item is created (by "clone" or the callback function), it is removed at the end of the move.
options.appendTo	Specifies the element in which the new element created with options.helper will be inserted during the time of the move. Possible values are a selector (only the first element in the list will be considered), a DOM element, or the string "parent" (parent element). The default is "parent".

Managing element movement

Table 10-2 describes the options for managing the actual movement of elements.

Table 10-2. Options for managing element movement

Option	Function
options.addClasses	When set to true (default), indicates that the ui-draggable and ui-dragga ble-dragging CSS classes should be added to the movable elements and the element being moved, respectively.
options.cursor	Specifies the cursor CSS property when the element moves. It represents the shape of the mouse pointer. The possible values are:
	• "auto" (default)
	• "crosshair" (across)
	• "default" (an arrow)
	• "pointer" (hand)
	• "move" (two arrows cross)
	• "e-resize" (expand to the right)
	• "ne-resize" (expand up right)
	• "nw-resize" (expand up left)
	• "n-resize" (expand up)
	• "se-resize" (expand down right)
	• "sw-resize" (expand down left)
	• "s-resize" (expand down)
	• "w-resize" (expand left)

Option	Function
	• "text" (pointer to write text)
	• "wait" (hourglass)
	• "help" (help pointer)
options.delay	Delay, in milliseconds, after which the first movement of the mouse is taken into account. The displacement may begin after that time. The default is 0.
options.distance	Number of pixels that the mouse must be moved before the displacement is taken into account. The default is 1 (i.e., a single pixel is enough to indicate that we want to move the item).
options.opacity	Opacity of the element moved when moving. The default is 1.
options.scope	String to restrict the drop of movable elements only on items that have the same options.scope (defined in droppable (options).
options.connectToSortable	Specifies a list whose elements are interchangeable. At the end of placement, the element is part of the list.

Managing the effect at the end of displacement

Once the element moved, it remains in its final position (default behavior). The options listed in Table 10-3 allow you to specify a new behavior of the element at the end of displacement (e.g., to return to its original position).

Table 10-3. Options for managing effects at the end of displacement

Option	Function
options.revert	Indicates whether the element is moved back to its original position at the end of the move.
	When set to true, the element returns to its original position. When set to false (the default), the element stays where it was dropped. When set to "valid", the element returns if it has been dropped on an element that accepts it, and when set to "invalid", the element returns if it has been dropped on an element that does not accept it.
options.revertDuration	Duration of displacement (in milliseconds) after which the element returns to its original position (see options.revert). By default, this period is 500 ms.

Managing displacement constraints

By default, elements can be moved anywhere on the page according to the movements of the mouse. We can change this default behavior using the options listed in Table 10-4.

Table 10-4. Options for managing displacement constraints

Option	Function
options.grid	Array [x, y] indicating the number of pixels that the element moves horizontally and vertically during displacement.
options.axis	Indicates an axis of movement ("x" horizontal, "y" vertical). The default is false (there is no specified axis, so displacement is possible in all directions).

Option	Function
`options.containment`	Indicates an element within which the displacement takes place. The element will be represented by a selector (only the first item in the list will be considered), a DOM element, or the string `"parent"` (parent element) or `"window"` (HTML page).
	It may also indicate an array [x1, y1, x2, y2] representing a rectangle formed by the points (x1, y1) and (x2, y2).
`options.snap`	Adjusts the display of the item being moved on other elements (which are flown). If you want to move an element to another, the displacement (in pixels) does not perfectly position the two elements one above the other.
	The value of this option is a selector indicating the elements for which the adjustment will be managed by jQuery UI (it adjusts the position of the displaced element to the position of the flown element if it is part of the selector). `true` indicates the `".ui-dragga ble"` selector—the moved element adjusts to all those that can be displaced. The default value is `false` (no adjustment).
`options.snapMode`	Specifies how the adjustment should be made between the moved element and those indicated in `options.snap`. `"inner"` specifies that the adjustment is made with the interior elements, `"outer"` indicates outside elements, and `"both"` specifies interior and exterior elements. The default value is `"both"`.
`options.snapTolerance`	Maximum number of pixels in the difference in position necessary to establish the adjustment. By default, this number is 20, meaning that as soon as 20 pixels separate the moved element from those in `options.snap`, the adjustment is made to the display, according to `options.snapMode`.

Managing window scroll

It is possible to move an element to locations on the page that are not in the visible part of the display. To do this, you can configure the page to scroll during item movement. Table 10-5 lists the options for managing scrolling.

Table 10-5. Options for managing window scrolling

Option	Function
`options.scroll`	When set to `true` (the default), the display will scroll if the item is moved outside the viewable area of the window.
`options.scrollSensitivity`	Indicates how many pixels the mouse must exit the window to cause scrolling of the display. The default is 20 pixels. This option is used only when `options.scroll` is set to `true`.
`options.scrollSpeed`	Indicates the scrolling speed of the display once scrolling begins. The default is 20.

Managing movable element events

Events associated with movable elements manage the beginning and end of the displacement and the displacement itself. Each of the methods associated with these events has two parameters: event is the mouse event and ui is a {helper, position, offset} object, the properties of which are described in Table 10-6. The options are listed in Table 10-7.

Table 10-6. Properties of the ui {helper, position, offset} object

Property	Function
ui.helper	jQuery class object associated with the element that moves (the element that was clicked or specified in options.helper).
ui.position	If the moved element is indicated in options.helper, this indicates the {top, left} position of the element relative to the edges of the page. Otherwise (if you move the element that was clicked), it indicates the displacement from the initial position of the element, considered to be (0, 0).
ui.offset	Indicates in all cases the {top, left} position of the moved element relative to the edges of the page.

Table 10-7. Managing events for movable elements

Option	Function
options.start	The start (event, ui) method is called when the displacement begins (the element has been clicked and the mouse was moved slightly).
options.drag	The drag (event, ui) method is called when the displacement continues after the first move.
options.stop	The stop (event, ui) method is called when the move is complete (the mouse button was released).

The draggable ("action", params) Method

The draggable ("action", params) method can perform an action on the movable elements, such as to prevent displacement. The action is specified as a string in the first argument (e.g., "disable" to prevent the displacement). The actions for this method are listed in Table 10-8.

Table 10-8. The draggable ("action", params) actions

Action	Function
draggable ("disable")	Disable drag management. Elements cannot be moved until the next call to the draggable ("enable") method.
draggable ("enable")	Reactivate drag management. The elements can be moved again.
draggable ("option", param)	Retrieve the value of the indicated param option. This option corresponds to one of those used with draggable (options).
draggable ("option", param, value)	Changes the value of the param option. This option corresponds to one of those used with draggable (options).
draggable ("destroy")	Remove drag management. The elements are no longer movable.

Event Management on the Moved Elements with bind ()

In addition to event methods offered in the options of the draggable (options) method, jQuery UI allows us to manage these events using the bind () method (detailed in Table 10-9).

Table 10-9. Events created by jQuery UI

Event	Function
dragstart	Same meaning as options.start.
drag	Same meaning as options.drag.
dragstop	Same meaning as options.stop.

Examples of Using Drag Functionality

In this section, we'll try out some of the drag functionality discussed in this chapter.

Carrying Out a Treatment When Moving

Let's display the coordinates of an element as it is being moved (Figure 10-1):

```
<script src = jquery.js></script>
<script src = jqueryui/js/jquery-ui-1.8.16.custom.min.js></script>

<link rel=stylesheet type=text/css
      href=jqueryui/css/smoothness/jquery-ui-1.8.16.custom.css />

<div id=div1 style="border:solid 1px;background-color:gainsboro;">
  <span>Item 1 to move</span><br /><br />
  <span>Item 2 to move</span><br /><br />
  <span>Item 3 to move</span>
</div>

<p>Start : <span id=start></span></p>
<p>Drag : <span id=drag></span></p>
<p>Stop : <span id=stop></span></p>

<script>

$("#div1 span").draggable ({
  start : function (event, ui)
  {
    $("#start").text (ui.offset.top + ", " + ui.offset.left);
  },
  drag : function (event, ui)
  {
    $("#drag").text (ui.offset.top + ", " + ui.offset.left);
  },
  stop : function (event, ui)
  {
```

```
        $("#stop").text (ui.offset.top + ", " + ui.offset.left);
    }
});

</script>
```

The first displacement causes the start, while the movements that follow are managed by the drag event. When the mouse is released, the stop event is triggered.

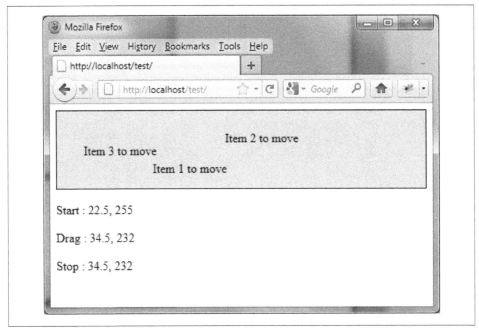

Figure 10-1. Coordinates of the drag

Imposing Limits on Displacement

You can limit the movement of elements on the screen. Here, we'll look at the various possible constraints.

Constraining the displacement to a given space

Here, we'll add onto the previous example by preventing <span> elements to be moved outside the parent <div>. Currently, no constraints are specified, which allows us to move any element using the draggable (options) method anywhere on the page:

```
<script src = jquery.js></script>
<script src = jqueryui/js/jquery-ui-1.8.16.custom.min.js></script>

<link rel=stylesheet type=text/css
      href=jqueryui/css/smoothness/jquery-ui-1.8.16.custom.css />
```

```
<div id=div1 style="border:solid 1px;background-color:gainsboro;">
  <span>Item 1 to move</span><br /><br />
  <span>Item 2 to move</span><br /><br />
  <span>Item 3 to move</span>
</div>

<script>

$("#div1 span").draggable ({
  containment : "#div1"
});

</script>
```

The containment option specifies the constraint of displacement. Here, <span> elements are prevented from going outside a <div> whose ID is div1 (Figure 10-2).

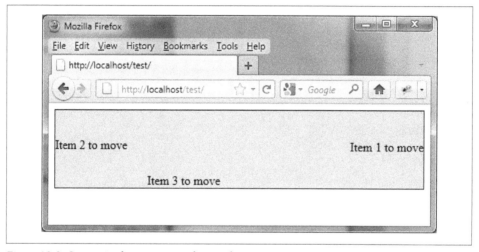

Figure 10-2. Constrained movement within a <div>

As this <div> is also the parent of movable elements, this constraint can also be written as follows:

```
containment : "parent"
```

It is also possible to impose constraints on horizontal or vertical movement, as we see in the following section.

Constraining the displacement horizontally or vertically

We can impose constraints on vertical or horizontal motion using options.axis worth "x" or "y". For example, to require that <span> elements can only move horizontally, we write the following code (shown in bold):

```
<script src = jquery.js></script>
<script src = jqueryui/js/jquery-ui-1.8.16.custom.min.js></script>
```

```
<link rel=stylesheet type=text/css
      href=jqueryui/css/smoothness/jquery-ui-1.8.16.custom.css />

<div id=div1 style="border:solid 1px;background-color:gainsboro;">
  <span>Item 1 to move</span><br /><br />
  <span>Item 2 to move</span><br /><br />
  <span>Item 3 to move</span>
</div>

<script>

$("#div1 span").draggable ({
  axis : "x"
});

</script>
```

To prevent movement of these items outside of the `<div>` parent, we need to add options.containment:

```
<script>

$("#div1 span").draggable ({
  axis : "x",
  containment : "parent"
});

</script>
```

Moving an Object by Duplicating

Here, we want to move an item that is the clone of the selected element (Figure 10-3). This is done using the options.helper option, value "clone":

```
<script src = jquery.js></script>
<script src = jqueryui/js/jquery-ui-1.8.16.custom.min.js></script>

<link rel=stylesheet type=text/css
      href=jqueryui/css/smoothness/jquery-ui-1.8.16.custom.css />

<div id=div1 style="border:solid 1px;background-color:gainsboro;">
  <span>Item 1 to move</span><br /><br />
  <span>Item 2 to move</span><br /><br />
  <span>Item 3 to move</span>
</div>

<script>

$("#div1 span").draggable ({
  helper : "clone"
});

</script>
```

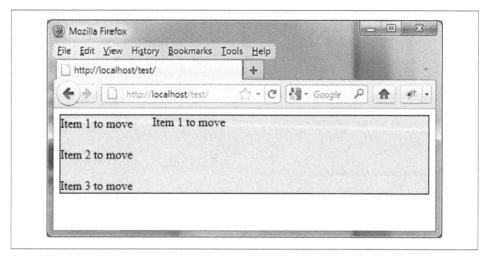

Figure 10-3. Moving a cloned item

In Figure 10-3, the first element is being dragged—only the cloned element is moved, while the original item remains in its original position. If you release the mouse, the cloned element disappears and the original item is still in its original position (Figure 10-4). The duplicate item is effectively moved and is removed from the DOM tree at the end of the move.

Figure 10-4. The original item remains in its original position.

We now want to keep the dragged item on the page. For this, we must create a new element that it is the same as the moved element and that keeps its position on the page at the end of the movement (Figure 10-5):

```
<script src = jquery.js></script>
<script src = jqueryui/js/jquery-ui-1.8.16.custom.min.js></script>
```

```
<link rel=stylesheet type=text/css
    href=jqueryui/css/smoothness/jquery-ui-1.8.16.custom.css />

<div id=div1 style="border:solid 1px;background-color:gainsboro;">
  <span>Item 1 to move</span><br /><br />
  <span>Item 2 to move</span><br /><br />
  <span>Item 3 to move</span>
</div>

<script>

$("#div1 span").draggable ({
  helper : "clone",
  stop : function (event, ui)
  {
    ui.helper.clone ().appendTo ($(this).parent ());
  }
});

</script>
```

At the end of the displacement (the stop () method), we duplicate the moved element (with ui.helper.clone ()) and insert it into the page at the same level as the moved <span> (with appendTo ()).

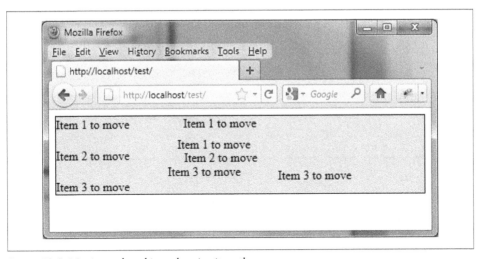

Figure 10-5. Moving a cloned item, keeping it on the page

Every time we move one of the <span> elements, we create a copy of the item, which explains the presence of several identical elements on the page.

Next, we can improve this script by preventing duplicates of the same element by removing the original. At the end of the displacement, the original item disappears (it is replaced by the one that was moved):

```
<script src = jquery.js></script>
<script src = jqueryui/js/jquery-ui-1.8.16.custom.min.js></script>

<link rel=stylesheet type=text/css
      href=jqueryui/css/smoothness/jquery-ui-1.8.16.custom.css />

<div id=div1 style="border:solid 1px;background-color:gainsboro;">
  <span>Item 1 to move</span><br /><br />
  <span>Item 2 to move</span><br /><br />
  <span>Item 3 to move</span>
</div>

<script>

$("#div1 span").draggable ({
  helper : "clone",
  stop : function (event, ui)
  {
    ui.helper.clone ().appendTo ($(this).parent ());
    $(this).remove ();
  }
});

</script>
```

The $(this).remove () statement deletes the original item at the end of the displacement.

The result of this script is shown in Figure 10-6.

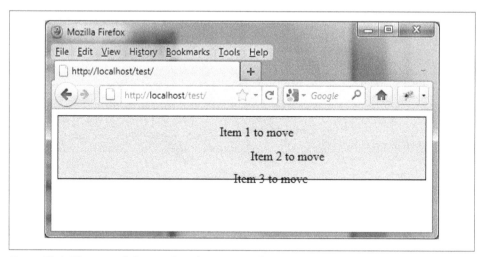

Figure 10-6. The original elements have been removed

However, each moved item is no longer draggable! Indeed, we have inserted a new (cloned) element on the page, but it does not have the characteristics of a draggable element. To allow movement of this element, we can call the draggable () method.

Consequently, moved items will be cloned, but may continue to be displaced by being cloned again:

```
<script src = jquery.js></script>
<script src = jqueryui/js/jquery-ui-1.8.16.custom.min.js></script>

<link rel=stylesheet type=text/css
      href=jqueryui/css/smoothness/jquery-ui-1.8.16.custom.css />

<div id=div1 style="border:solid 1px;background-color:gainsboro;">
  <span>Item 1 to move</span><br /><br />
  <span>Item 2 to move</span><br /><br />
  <span>Item 3 to move</span>
</div>

<script>

$("#div1 span").draggable ({
  helper : "clone"
}).bind ("dragstop", f = function (event, ui)
{
  ui.helper.clone ()
          .appendTo ($(this).parent ())
          .draggable ( { helper : "clone" } )
          .bind ("dragstop", f);
  $(this).remove ();
});

</script>
```

Here, we use the `dragstop` event instead of the `stop ()` method used previously. Indeed, it is necessary for the cloned item to use this event handler, so the easiest way to pass it is to use the `bind ("dragstop", f)` method, where the `f` function is the callback function used previously.

The droppable () Method

The `droppable ()` method manages elements of the HTML page on which you want to drop a moved item. This method can be used in two forms:

- `$(selector, context).droppable (options)`
- `$(selector, context).droppable ("action", params)`

The droppable (options) Method

The `droppable (options)` method declares that an HTML element can be used as an element in which to deposit other elements. The `options` parameter is an object for specifying the behavior of the involved elements.

The elements of deposit are those from the list associated with the selector for which the `droppable (options)` method is called. These `options` primarily define which elements can be dropped on these elements of deposit, and the behavior of elements when a drop is made.

Managing the behavior of the elements of deposit

Table 10-10 describes the options for the `droppable (options)` method.

Table 10-10. Options for managing deposit elements

Option	Function
`options.disabled`	When set to `true`, disables movement of item over the specified elements and the drop into those elements. If items pass over an unauthorized element, the drop will not be considered until these elements are enabled (by using `droppable ("enable")`).
`options.tolerance`	Indicates how the draggable element should cover the element of deposit for the drop being accepted. The possible values are `"fit"` (the draggable element covers the element of deposit in full), `"intersect"` (half), `"touch"` (touching), and `"point"` (the mouse has entered the element of deposit). The default is `"intersect"`.
`options.addClasses`	When set to `true` (the default), the `ui-droppable` CSS class must be added to the list elements.

Indicating which elements can be dropped

By default, all draggable elements can be deposited on an element of deposit. It is possible to state exactly which draggable elements are accepted, using the options listed in Table 10-11.

Table 10-11. Options for specifying elements that can be deposited

Option	Function
`options.accept`	Indicates elements accepted for the deposit. It is a selector or a callback function called for each of the draggable elements in the page (of the form `accept (element)`, in which `element` corresponds to a draggable element). The function should return `true` if the deposited element is accepted. The default selector is `"*"`, meaning that every item is accepted for deposit.
`options.scope`	String used to restrict the deposit of draggable elements only to items that have the same `options.scope` (defined in `draggable (options)`). The items for which the deposit will be accepted are those defined in `options.accept` that also satisfy `options.scope`.

Managing the appearance of elements of deposit

You can add CSS classes to the elements of deposit to change the style of the elements depending on conditions that you specify. These options are listed in Table 10-12.

Table 10-12. Options for managing the appearance of the elements of deposit

Option	Function
options.hoverClass	String representing one or more CSS classes to be added to the element of deposit when an accepted element (an element indicated in options.accept) moves into it.
options.activeClass	String representing one or more CSS classes to be added to the element of deposit when an accepted element (one of those indicated in options.accept) is being dragged (not necessarily into the element of deposit).

Managing events on the elements of deposit

Events associated with elements of deposit are used to manage the beginning and end of the movement of an accepted element and the deposit of the element itself. Each of the methods associated with these events has two parameters: event corresponds to the mouse event (listed in Table 10-13), and ui is a {draggable, helper, offset} object (described in Table 10-14).

Table 10-13. Options for managing events

Option	Function
options.activate	The activate (event, ui) method is called when the movement of an accepted element starts (the element was clicked and the mouse was moved slightly).
options.deactivate	The deactivate (event, ui) method is called when movement of an accepted element ends (the mouse was released).
options.over	The over (event, ui) method is called when an accepted element is on top of the element of deposit (as defined in options.tolerance).
options.out	The out (event, ui) method is called when an accepted element leaves the element of deposit (as defined in options.tolerance).
options.drop	The drop (event, ui) method is called when an accepted element is dropped on the element of deposit (the mouse was released).

Table 10-14. Properties of the ui {draggable, helper, offset} object

Property	Function
ui.draggable	jQuery class object associated with the item that was clicked to move it (but not necessarily the element that moves, if we use options.helper in the draggable (options) method).
ui.helper	jQuery class object associated with the element that moves (but not necessarily the element that was clicked, if options.helper is used in draggable (options)).
ui.offset	In all cases, indicates the {top, left} position of the element moved relative to the edges of the page.

The droppable ("action", params) Method

The `droppable ("action", params)` method can perform an action on elements of deposit such as inhibiting the deposit. The action is specified as a string in the first argument (e.g., `"disable"` to prevent the deposit). These actions are listed in Table 10-15.

Table 10-15. The droppable ("action", params) method actions

Action	Function
droppable ("disable")	Disable the deposit operation. The elements are no longer elements of deposit.
droppable ("enable")	Reactivate the deposit operation. The elements can again receive a deposit.
droppable ("option", param)	Retrieve the value of the indicated `param` option. This option corresponds to one of those used with `droppable (options)`.
droppable ("option", param, value)	Set the value of the indicated `param` option. This option corresponds to one of those used with `droppable (options)`.
droppable ("destroy")	Remove the management of the deposit. The elements are no longer elements of deposit.

Event Management on the Elements of Deposit with bind ()

In addition to event methods offered in the options of the `droppable (options)` method, jQuery UI allows us to manage these events using the `bind ()` method. The events of this method are described in Table 10-16.

Table 10-16. Events created by jQuery UI

Event	Function
dropactivate	Same meaning as `options.activate`.
dropdeactivate	Same meaning as `options.deactivate`.
dropover	Same meaning as `options.over`.
dropout	Same meaning as `options.out`.
drop	Same meaning as `options.drop`.

Examples of Using the Drop Functionality: A Shopping Cart

With the help of a shopping cart, let's examine the various possibilities of the drop functionality.

Creating a Shopping Cart with Drag-and-Drop

Let's use drop functionality to manage a shopping cart of books. Books are displayed as images, which users can drag into a cart for purchase (Figure 10-7). Each book can be moved, and the cart is a place for depositing books. Once the book is placed in the cart, it is positioned to the right of the cart (Figure 10-8):

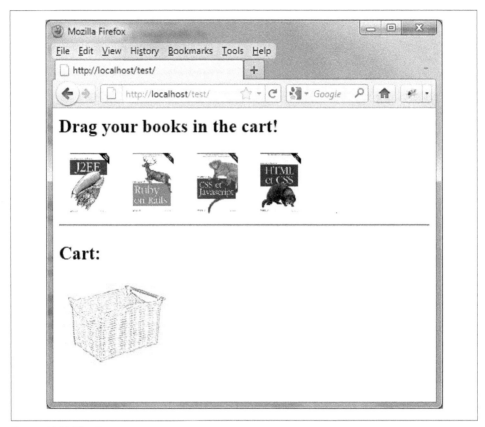

Figure 10-7. The shopping cart is empty

```
<script src=jquery.js></script>
<script src=jqueryui/development-bundle/ui/jquery-ui-1.8.4.custom.js></script>

<link rel=stylesheet type=text/css
    href="jqueryui/development-bundle/themes/smoothness/jquery.ui.all.css" />

<h2> Drag your books in the cart! </h2>
<div id=books>
  <img src=images/j2ee.jpg height=80 />
  <img src=images/rails.jpg height=80 />
  <img src=images/javascript.jpg height=80 />
  <img src=images/html.jpg height=80 />
</div>

<hr />

<h2> Cart: </h2>
```

```
<div id=shopping>
  <img src=images/basket.jpg class=basket />
</div>

<script>

$("div#books img").draggable ({
  revert : "invalid"
});

$("div#shopping img.basket").droppable ({
  drop : function (event, ui)
  {
    $("div#shopping").append (ui.draggable);
    $(ui.draggable).css ({ position:"relative", top:"0px", left:"0px" })
               .draggable ("disable")
               .css ({ opacity : 1 });
  }
});

</script>
```

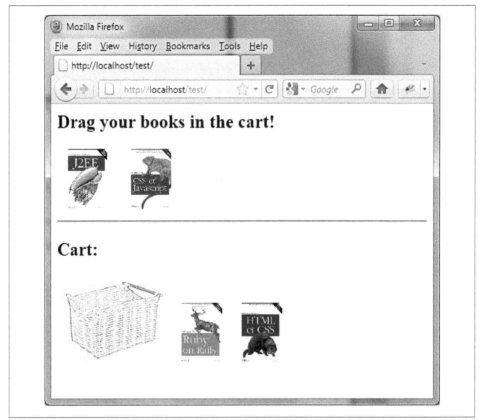

Figure 10-8. The shopping cart contains two books

$("""div#books img"").draggable ()makes each picture draggable, while the cart is defined as an element of deposit with $("div#shopping img.basket").droppable (). The revert option "invalid" resets the dragged item to its original position if it is not placed in the cart.

The drop () method allows treatment when depositing a book in the cart. The moved image (ui.draggable) is inserted at the end of the cart (by append ()). The css () instruction removes the book picture from its original position and gives it a new position to the right of the basket. The draggable ("disable") instruction prevents users from moving this image again and gives it an opacity of 1 (because the draggable ("disable") instruction automatically decreases the opacity of the element).

Adding a Visual Effect to Shopping Cart Deposits

When a book picture is dragged onto the shopping cart, there is no visual indication that anything will happen if the picture is dropped there.

Let's modify the code so that the cart appears responsive when books are deposited in it, for example, by displaying a red border (Figure 10-9):

```
<script src = jquery.js></script>
<script src = jqueryui/js/jquery-ui-1.8.16.custom.min.js></script>

<link rel=stylesheet type=text/css
      href=jqueryui/css/smoothness/jquery-ui-1.8.16.custom.css />

<style type=text/css>
  .basket {
    border : transparent solid 2px;
  }
  .hover {
    border-color : red;
  }
</style>

<h2> Drag your books in the cart! </h2>
<div id=books>
  <img src=images/j2ee.jpg height=80 />
  <img src=images/rails.jpg height=80 />
  <img src=images/javascript.jpg height=80 />
  <img src=images/html.jpg height=80 />
</div>

<hr />

<h2> Cart: </h2>
<div id=shopping>
  <img src=images/basket.jpg class=basket />
</div>

<script>
```

```
$("div#books img").draggable ({
  revert : "invalid"
});

$("div#shopping img.basket").droppable ({
  hoverClass : "hover",
  drop : function (event, ui)
  {
    $("div#shopping").append (ui.draggable);
    $(ui.draggable).css ({ position:"relative", top:"0px", left:"0px" })
                   .draggable ("disable")
                   .css ({ opacity : 1 });
  }
});

</script>
```

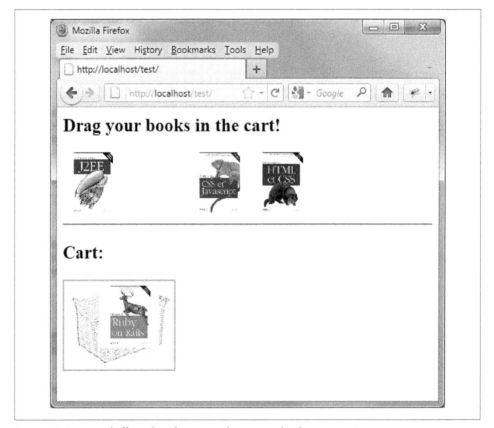

Figure 10-9. A visual effect when depositing elements in the shopping cart

We have added the hoverClass option to the script in the droppable (options) method. This allows you to specify one or more CSS classes that will be added to the element of deposit when an authorized element moves over it. This class includes the border-color:red CSS instruction. For this to work, we have included CSS instructions in the basket class (used by the element of deposit, that is to say the shopping cart) for a transparent border, which avoids having a displacement of the shopping cart when moving an item onto it (which would add a border).

Removing an Item from the Cart

The books in the shopping cart may not, at present, be removed from it. Here, we'll change the code to allow users to remove books from the cart. When books are removed from the cart, they re-enter the list of books to buy. To do this, we manage the depositing of a purchased book on the <div> containing the list of books to buy (div#books):

```
<script src = jquery.js></script>
<script src = jqueryui/js/jquery-ui-1.8.16.custom.min.js></script>

<link rel=stylesheet type=text/css
      href=jqueryui/css/smoothness/jquery-ui-1.8.16.custom.css />

<style type=text/css>
  .basket {
    border : transparent solid 2px;
  }
  .hover {
    border-color : red;
  }
</style>

<h2> Drag your books in the cart! </h2>
<div id=books>
  <img src=images/j2ee.jpg height=80 />
  <img src=images/rails.jpg height=80 />
  <img src=images/javascript.jpg height=80 />
  <img src=images/html.jpg height=80 />
</div>

<hr />

<h2> Cart: </h2>
<div id=shopping>
  <img src=images/basket.jpg class=basket />
</div>

<script>

$("div#books img").draggable ({
  revert : "invalid"
});

$("div#shopping img.basket").droppable ({
  hoverClass : "hover",
  drop : function (event, ui)
  {
    $("div#shopping").append (ui.draggable);
```

```
      $(ui.draggable).css ({ position:"relative", top:"0px", left:"0px" })
                    .addClass ("bought");
  }
});

$("div#books").droppable ({
  accept : ".bought",
  drop : function (event, ui)
  {
    $("div#books").append (ui.draggable);
    $(ui.draggable).css ({ position:"relative", top:"0px", left:"0px" })
              .removeClass ("bought");
  }
});

</script>
```

Each book placed in the cart is now assigned the "bought" CSS class. The div#books will only accept books that have this class (thanks to accept sets to ".bought"). The drop () method used in the list of books is similar to that used on the cart, except that it removes the "bought" CSS class, because the book is no longer in the shopping cart.

Selecting Items

jQuery UI makes it easy to select items on the page. *Select* means that the page elements can be grouped in the same block to be processed simultaneously (e.g., selecting several files to put them in the trash). Rather than putting them one by one into the trash (using the drag-and-drop functionality that we examined in Chapter 10), items are selected using the mouse and then dragged together to the trash.

jQuery UI has implemented this functionality in a similar way to that found in graphical operating systems such as Windows, Mac OS, or Linux. You can use the mouse to select multiple items and also select or deselect an individual item in the group by pressing the Ctrl key while you click.

Basic Principles of Selecting Items

Suppose we want to write the HTML code to display the selection shown in Figure 11-1. Here, we have five paragraphs and we selected the first three with the mouse. A dotted rectangle is added during mouse movement, showing the selection area.

The selectable items should be grouped together in a `<div>` (or any other parent). All elements in the descendants of that parent can be selected.

In the `<script>` tag, the encompassing `<div>` element is managed by the jQuery UI `selectable ()` method:

```
<script src = jquery.js></script>
<script src = jqueryui/js/jquery-ui-1.8.16.custom.min.js></script>

<link rel=stylesheet type=text/css
      href=jqueryui/css/smoothness/jquery-ui-1.8.16.custom.css />

<div id=div1>
  <p> Paragraph 1 </p>
  <p> Paragraph 2 </p>
  <p> Paragraph 3 </p>
  <p> Paragraph 4 </p>
  <p> Paragraph 5 </p>
```

```
</div>

<script>

$("#div1").selectable ();

</script>
```

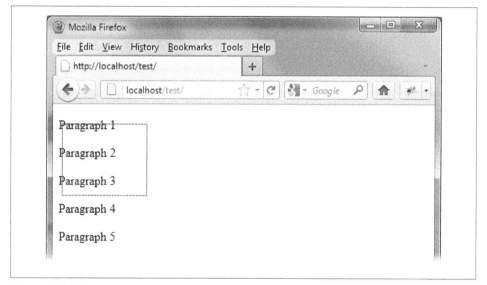

Figure 11-1. Selecting items in an HTML page

Formatting Content

The `selectable ()` method displays a dotted rectangle symbolizing the selection. In addition, it adds new CSS classes to HTML elements that are selectable as well as those selected.

In Figure 11-2, for example, the HTML generated by jQuery UI after the `selectable ()` method changed the HTML (the code was recovered using the Firebug extension in Firefox).

The encompassing `<div>` element was assigned the `ui-selectable` CSS class, whereas selectable items it contains have the `ui-selectee` class. The first three paragraphs being selected have the `ui-selecting` class. Once the mouse button is released, the selected paragraphs will then have the `ui-selected` class (instead of `ui-selecting`).

Notice that a `<div>` was created by jQuery UI (`ui-selectable-helper` class), which is the dotted rectangle representing the selection. This `<div>` will be removed from the page when the mouse button is released.

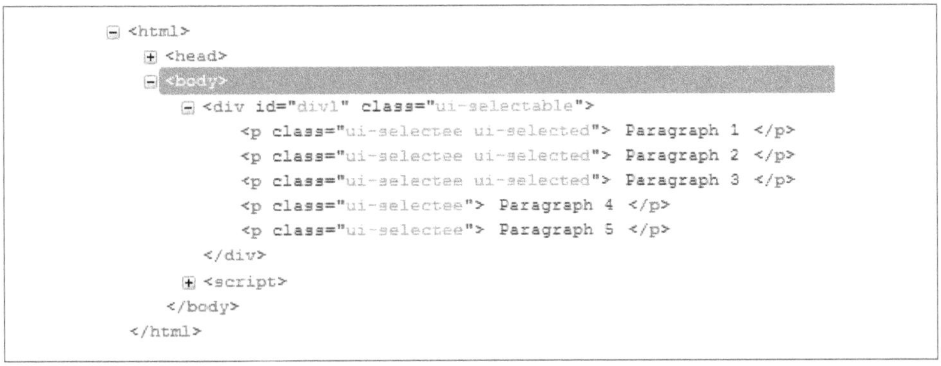

```
⊟ <html>
    ⊞ <head>
    ⊟ <body>
        ⊟ <div id="div1" class="ui-selectable">
              <p class="ui-selectee ui-selected"> Paragraph 1 </p>
              <p class="ui-selectee ui-selected"> Paragraph 2 </p>
              <p class="ui-selectee ui-selected"> Paragraph 3 </p>
              <p class="ui-selectee"> Paragraph 4 </p>
              <p class="ui-selectee"> Paragraph 5 </p>
          </div>
        ⊞ <script>
      </body>
    </html>
```

Figure 11-2. HTML generated by the selectable () method

You can use CSS classes of elements to customize the display. For example, if we change the CSS classes ui-selecting and ui-selected associated with <p> elements, we should get a new look for items being selected and deselected.

Modify these elements in the HTML by adding a <style> tag so that the rectangle and the selected paragraphs are displayed with a solid red line (Figure 11-3). When the mouse is released, the selected paragraphs will be displayed on light gray background (Figure 11-4):

```
<script src = jquery.js></script>
<script src = jqueryui/js/jquery-ui-1.8.16.custom.min.js></script>

<link rel=stylesheet type=text/css
      href=jqueryui/css/smoothness/jquery-ui-1.8.16.custom.css />

<style type=text/css>
  p.ui-selecting {
    color : red;
  }
  p.ui-selected {
    background-color : gainsboro;
  }
  div.ui-selectable-helper {
    border-color : red;
    border-style : solid;
  }
</style>

<div id=div1>
  <p> Paragraph 1 </p>
  <p> Paragraph 2 </p>
  <p> Paragraph 3 </p>
  <p> Paragraph 4 </p>
  <p> Paragraph 5 </p>
</div>

<script>
```

```
$("#div1").selectable ();

</script>
```

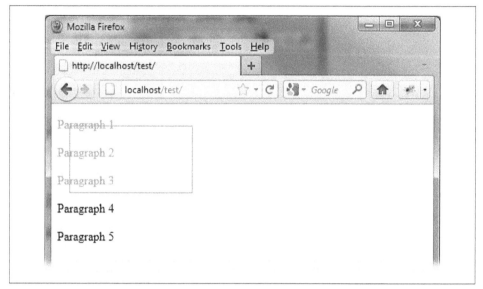

Figure 11-3. Customized display of the selection in progress

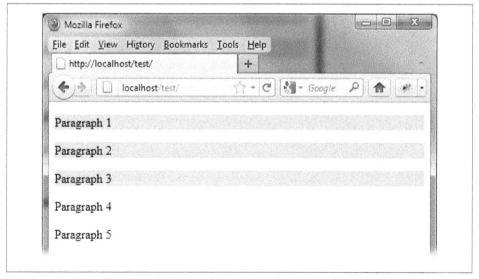

Figure 11-4. Customized selected items

Users can select or deselect any of paragraphs by pressing the Ctrl key while clicking an item with the mouse. For example, users can select the fifth paragraph and deselect the second and fourth, as shown in Figure 11-5.

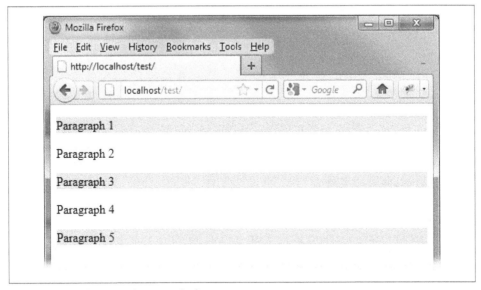

Figure 11-5. A change in the original selection

The selectable () Method

The selectable () method can be used in two forms:

- $(selector, context).selectable (options)
- $(selector, context).selectable ("action", params)

The selectable (options) Method

The selectable (options) method declares that an HTML element contains selectable items. The options parameter specifies behavior when selecting.

Managing selected items

All items that are in the descendants of the elements on which the selectable (options) method applies are selectable and inherit the ui-selectee CSS class (whether selected or not). The options listed in Table 11-1 allow you to filter the elements of the descendants to indicate those that will actually be selectable.

Table 11-1. Options for specifying the selectable elements

Option	Function
options.disabled	When set to true, disables the selection mechanism. Users cannot select the elements until the mechanism is restored using the selectable ("enable") instruction.
options.filter	Selector indicating which elements can be part of the selection. These will inherit the ui-selectee class and will be selectable. By default, the selector is "*" (all the elements of the descendants can be selected).
options.cancel	Selector indicating the elements on which it is forbidden to start the selection (but may be part of the selection).
options.distance	Distance (in pixels) the mouse must move to consider the selection in progress. This is useful, for example, to prevent simple clicks from being interpreted as a group selection.
	The default value is 0, thus allowing a simple click on an item to select or deselect it.

Managing events on selected items

The options listed in Table 11-2 let you manage events that occur on selected items, such as the selection or deselection of an item. The first usage example below shows the order in which these events appear on the page.

Table 11-2. Options for managing events on selected items

Option	Function
options.start	The start (event) method is called whenever the mouse is clicked in the element that uses the selectable (options) method. It then starts a selection sequence (for which selected or deselected items are added to the previous selection).
options.stop	The stop (event) method is called when the mouse has been released. The selection sequence is complete.
options.selecting	The selecting (event, ui) method is called when a new item has been selected and the mouse has not yet been released (the stop () method has not yet been called for this selection sequence). The DOM element being selected is recorded in ui.selecting.
options.unselecting	The unselecting (event, ui) method is called when a new item has been deselected and the mouse has not yet been released (the stop () method has not yet been called for this selection sequence). The DOM element being deselected is recorded in ui.unselecting.
options.selected	The selected (event, ui) method is called for each of the items selected in the selection sequence when the mouse is released. Any previously selected items do not cause the call to this method (although they remain selected). The selected DOM element is in ui.selected.
options.unselected	The unselected (event) method is called for each element deselected in this selection sequence when the mouse is released. Any previously deselected items do not cause the call to this method (although they remain deselected). The deselected DOM element is recorded in ui.unselected.

We define the term *selection sequence* as all the methods called from `options.start` to `options.stop` included. In each method, the `this` value refers to the element item that calls the `selectable (options)` method (that is to say, the one with the `ui-selectable` CSS class).

The selectable ("action", params) Method

The `selectable ("action", params)` method can perform an action on selectable items, such as authorizing the selection. The action is specified as a string in the first argument (e.g., `"disable"` to inhibit the operation). These actions are listed in Table 11-3).

Table 11-3. The selectable ("action", params) method actions

Action	Function
selectable ("disable")	Deactivate the selection operation.
selectable ("enable")	Reactivate the selection operation.
selectable ("option", param)	Retrieve the value of the param option. This option corresponds to one of those used with selectable (options).
selectable ("option", param, value)	Change the value of the param option. This option corresponds to one of those used with selectable (options).
electable ("destroy")	Remove the management of the selection.

Event Management in the Selection with bind ()

In addition to event methods proposed in the options of the `selectable (options)` method, jQuery UI allows us to manage these events using the `bind ()` method. These events are listed in Table 11-4.

Table 11-4. Events created by jQuery UI

Event	Function
selectablestart	Same meaning as options.start.
selectablestop	Same meaning as options.stop.
selectableselecting	Same meaning as options.selecting.
selectableunselecting	Same meaning as options.unselecting.
selectableselected	Same meaning as options.selected.
selectableunselected	Same meaning as options.unselected.

Examples of Using the Selection Mechanism

Let's apply the information presented in this chapter. Here, we'll create examples that incorporate the selection mechanism.

Displaying the Order of the Events During the Selection

The goal in this example is to display the order of the events described above (shown in Figure 11-6). For this, we display five selectable paragraphs and a `<span>` element containing the name of events. The start event is shown in bold to indicate the beginning of a new sequence:

```
<script src = jquery.js></script>
<script src = jqueryui/js/jquery-ui-1.8.16.custom.min.js></script>

<link rel=stylesheet type=text/css
      href=jqueryui/css/smoothness/jquery-ui-1.8.16.custom.css />

<style type=text/css>
  p.ui-selecting {
    color : red;
  }
  p.ui-selected {
    background-color : gainsboro;
  }
</style>

<div id=div1>
  <p> Paragraph 1 </p>
  <p> Paragraph 2 </p>
  <p> Paragraph 3 </p>
  <p> Paragraph 4 </p>
  <p> Paragraph 5 </p>
</div>

<hr />

<span id=result></span>

<script>

$("#div1").selectable ({
  start : function (event)
  {
    $("span#result").html ($("span#result").html () + " <b>start</b>");
  },
  stop : function (event)
  {
    $("span#result").html ($("span#result").html () + ", stop");
  },
  selecting : function (event, ui)
  {
    $("span#result").html ($("span#result").html () + ", selecting");
  },
  unselecting : function (event, ui)
  {
    $("span#result").html ($("span#result").html () + ", unselecting");
  },
  selected : function (event, ui)
  {
```

```
    $("span#result").html ($("span#result").html () + ", selected");
  },
  unselected : function (event, ui)
  {
    $("span#result").html ($("span#result").html () + ", unselected");
  }
});

</script>
```

At each event, the previous contents of <span> are recovered and the name of the called method is added.

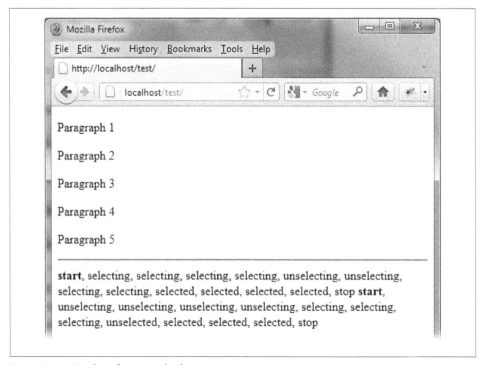

Figure 11-6. Display after several selection sequences

Preventing the Selection of an Element

By default, all elements of the descendants can be selected. The `filter` option is a selector to indicate precisely those we would like users to be able to select. For example, to select only the first paragraph, write the following:

```
<script src = jquery.js></script>
<script src = jqueryui/js/jquery-ui-1.8.16.custom.min.js></script>

<link rel=stylesheet type=text/css
      href=jqueryui/css/smoothness/jquery-ui-1.8.16.custom.css />
```

```
<style type=text/css>
  p.ui-selecting {
    color : red;
  }
  p.ui-selected {
    background-color : gainsboro;
  }
</style>

<div id=div1>
  <p> Paragraph 1 </p>
  <p> Paragraph 2 </p>
  <p> Paragraph 3 </p>
  <p> Paragraph 4 </p>
  <p> Paragraph 5 </p>
</div>

<script>

$("#div1").selectable ({
  filter : "p:first-child"
});

</script>
```

We can see the display when trying to select all the paragraphs in Figure 11-7. Only the first paragraph can actually be selected, even if the attempted selection includes five paragraphs.

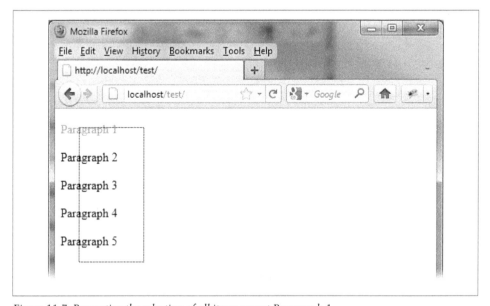

Figure 11-7. Preventing the selection of all items except Paragraph 1

Conversely, to prevent the selection of the first paragraph (shown in Figure 11-8) use the following:

```
<script>

$("#div1").selectable ({
  filter : "p:not(:first-child)"
});

</script>
```

Inhibiting Clicks to Select an Item

By default, a click on a selectable item is sufficient to select or deselect it. We can inhibit the ability to select an item by clicking on it, thereby requiring users to draw selection rectangles around the items they want to select. This is done using the `distance` option with a value greater than 0:

```
<script src = jquery.js></script>
<script src = jqueryui/js/jquery-ui-1.8.16.custom.min.js></script>

<link rel=stylesheet type=text/css
      href=jqueryui/css/smoothness/jquery-ui-1.8.16.custom.css />

<style type=text/css>
  p.ui-selecting {
    color : red;
  }
  p.ui-selected {
    background-color : gainsboro;
  }
</style>

<div id=div1>
  <p> Paragraph 1 </p>
  <p> Paragraph 2 </p>
  <p> Paragraph 3 </p>
  <p> Paragraph 4 </p>
  <p> Paragraph 5 </p>
</div>

<script>

$("#div1").selectable ({
  distance : 1
});

</script>
```

Paragraphs can now be selected by dragging the mouse in the encompassing `<div>` (and moving at least one pixel), so there is no possibility of using a single click to select an item. To restore this functionality, set `options.distance` to 0.

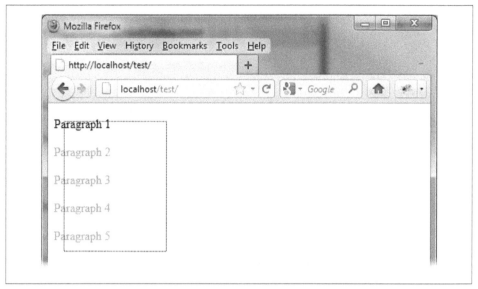

Figure 11-8. Preventing the selection of an element

Managing a Shopping Cart

Here, we'll build on the shopping cart example from Chapter 10 to allow users to select one or more books and drag them into the shopping cart. This will provide the opportunity to select several books for purchase with one mouse move (Figure 11-9).

This program takes into account some differences between Internet Explorer and other browsers. In particular, a problem arises in Internet Explorer when moving books to the cart—the move can be interpreted as a new selection sequence. To resolve this issue, we add the `isSelected` property (`true` if the book is selected) to each selected book. Other browsers use the `ui-selected` CSS class automatically added by jQuery UI when selecting an item. With this trick, our program is compatible:

```
<script src = jquery.js></script>
<script src = jqueryui/js/jquery-ui-1.8.16.custom.min.js></script>

<link rel=stylesheet type=text/css
      href=jqueryui/css/smoothness/jquery-ui-1.8.16.custom.css />

<style type=text/css>
  .basket {
    border : transparent solid 2px;
  }
  .hover {
    border-color : red;
  }
  img.border {
    border : transparent solid 2px;
```

```
    }
    img.ui-selected {
      border-color : red;
    }
</style>

<h2>Drag your books in the cart! </h2>
<div id=books>
  <img src=images/j2ee.jpg height=80 class=border />
  <img src=images/rails.jpg height=80 class=border />
  <img src=images/javascript.jpg height=80 class=border />
  <img src=images/html.jpg height=80 class=border />
</div>

<hr />

<h2> Cart: </h2>
<div id=shopping>
  <img src=images/basket.jpg class=basket />
</div>

<script>

$("div#shopping img.basket").droppable ({
  hoverClass : "hover",
  deactivate : function (event, ui)
  {
    var selector = $.browser.msie ?
                    "div#books img[isSelected=true]" :
                    "div#books img.ui-selected";
    $(selector).each (function (index)
    {
      $(this).css ({ position:"relative", top:"0px", left:"0px" });
    });
  },
  drop : function (event, ui)
  {
    var selector = $.browser.msie ?
                    "div#books img[isSelected=true]" :
                    "div#books img.ui-selected";
    $(selector).each (function (index)
    {
      $("div#shopping").append (this);
      $(this).css ({ position:"relative", top:"0px", left:"0px" })
             .removeClass ("ui-selected");
    });
  }
});

$("div#books").selectable ({
  selected : function (event, ui)
  {
    ui.selected.isSelected = true;
    $(ui.selected).draggable ({
      start : function (event)
```

```
            {
              $("div#books").selectable ("disable");
            },
            drag : function (event, ui)
            {
              var selector = $.browser.msie ?
                                  "div#books img[isSelected=true]" :
                                  "div#books img.ui-selected";
              $(selector).each (function (index)
              {
                $(this).css ({ position : "relative",
                               top : ui.helper.css ("top"),
                               left : ui.helper.css ("left") });
              });
            },
            stop : function (event)
            {
              $("div#books").selectable ("enable");
            }
          });
        },
        unselected : function (event, ui)
        {
          ui.unselected.isSelected = false;
          $(ui.unselected).draggable ("destroy");
        }
      });

    </script>
```

Figure 11-9. Three books are placed in the cart simultaneously

---

Permutation of Elements in the Page

Moving items to insert them elsewhere in the page has become indispensable in current web applications. Users move elements visually by dragging with the mouse, and the system automatically inserts the moved items. Here, everything is handled internally by jQuery UI, which provides us the mechanism that implements this functionality.

Here we call this operation a *permutation*, because the moved element leaves its place, while the destination (the location where the element is deposited) expands to allow the insertion of the new element.

Basic Principles of Permutation of Elements

Suppose we want to write the HTML code to display a paragraph being moved, as shown in Figure 12-1. Here, we have five paragraphs. The first is selected using the mouse and is moved from the list and inserted into a new location.

With jQuery UI, swappable elements must be inserted into a parent element (`<div>` or other). All elements in the descendants of this parent are permutable with each other.

To specify that these elements are permutable with the mouse in the HTML page, the jQuery UI `sortable ()` method manages the encompassing `<div>` in the `<script>`:

```
<script src = jquery.js></script>
<script src = jqueryui/js/jquery-ui-1.8.16.custom.min.js></script>

<link rel=stylesheet type=text/css
      href=jqueryui/css/smoothness/jquery-ui-1.8.16.custom.css />

<div id=div1>
  <p> Paragraph 1 </p>
  <p> Paragraph 2 </p>
  <p> Paragraph 3 </p>
  <p> Paragraph 4 </p>
  <p> Paragraph 5 </p>
</div>

<script>
```

```
$("#div1").sortable ();

</script>
```

Figure 12-1. Paragraph 1 is being moved

Formatting Content

The `sortable ()` method allows users to move the item selected by the mouse, and adds new CSS classes to the item being moved.

In Figure 12-2, for example, the `sortable ()` instruction changes the HTML and we start moving the first paragraph (this code was recovered by Firebug).

The encompassing `<div>` element is assigned the `ui-sortable` CSS class, while the paragraph being moved is assigned the `ui-sortable-helper` class. Notice that jQuery UI created a `<div>` (`ui-sortable-placeholder` class) corresponding to the place left vacant when the paragraph was moved. This `<div>` moves progressively and will be removed from the page when the mouse button is released.

We can use CSS classes to customize the display. For example, if we change the `ui-sortable-helper` CSS class associated with the element that moves, we get a new look for the item being moved.

Modify these elements in the HTML by adding a `<style>` tag so that the paragraph being moved is displayed in red, becoming black at the end of displacement (see Figure 12-3):

```
<script src = jquery.js></script>
<script src = jqueryui/js/jquery-ui-1.8.16.custom.min.js></script>
```

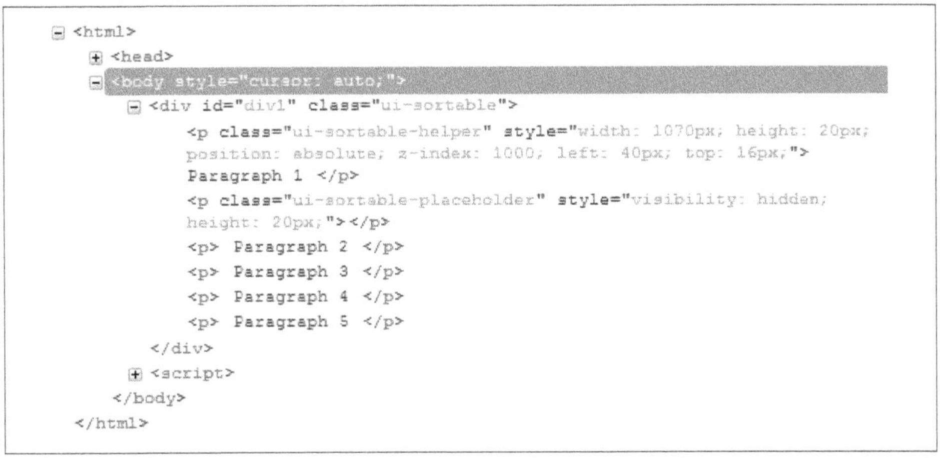

```
☐ <html>
   ⊞ <head>
   ☐ <body style="cursor: auto;">
      ☐ <div id="div1" class="ui-sortable">
          <p class="ui-sortable-helper" style="width: 1070px; height: 20px;
          position: absolute; z-index: 1000; left: 40px; top: 16px;">
          Paragraph 1 </p>
          <p class="ui-sortable-placeholder" style="visibility: hidden;
          height: 20px;"></p>
          <p> Paragraph 2 </p>
          <p> Paragraph 3 </p>
          <p> Paragraph 4 </p>
          <p> Paragraph 5 </p>
      </div>
   ⊞ <script>
   </body>
</html>
```

Figure 12-2. HTML generated by the sortable () method

```
<link rel=stylesheet type=text/css
      href=jqueryui/css/smoothness/jquery-ui-1.8.16.custom.css />

<style type=text/css>
  p.ui-sortable-helper {
    color : red;
  }
</style>

<div id=div1>
  <p> Paragraph 1 </p>
  <p> Paragraph 2 </p>
  <p> Paragraph 3 </p>
  <p> Paragraph 4 </p>
  <p> Paragraph 5 </p>
</div>

<script>

$("#div1").sortable ();

</script>
```

The sortable () Method

The sortable () method can be used in two forms:

- `$(selector, context).sortable (options)`
- `$(selector, context).sortable ("action", params)`

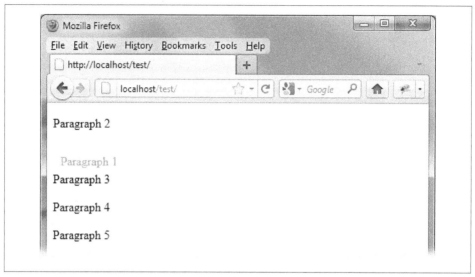

Figure 12-3. Customized elements

The sortable (options) Method

The sortable (options) method declares that an HTML element contains interchangeable elements. The options parameter is an object that specifies behavior in the permutation. Among the options available, many are similar to those we studied in the draggable (options) method (Chapter 10).

Specifying and managing the movable elements

The options listed in Table 12-1 allow you to indicate which items can be moved for switching. By default, all items that are in the descendants of the elements on which the sortable (options) method applies are movable. Use these options to inhibit the movement for all items or only some, or even move a new item created on the fly. Table 12-2 describes the options for managing the specified movable elements.

Table 12-1. Options for specifying the movable elements

Option	Function
options.disabled	When set to true, disables the movement of elements. No displacement or deposit of elements will be considered until these elements are returned enabled (using the sortable ("enable") instruction).
options.cancel	A selector representing the elements for which the displacement is prohibited. Users cannot start swapping by clicking on any of these items. This allows you to restrict the start list items (those on which the sortable (options) method applies).
options.helper	Indicates that we would like to move an element other than the one the mouse is pointing to.

Option	Function
	The `"clone"` value indicates that the item is duplicated and that it is the new element that moves, while the original remains in its original position.
	With `"original"` (default) is the initial element that is moved (default operation).
	If you specify a callback function, it creates and returns a new element that will be moved. In any case, if a new item is created (by `"clone"` or the callback function), it is removed at the end of the move.
options.appendTo	Specifies the element in which the new element created with `options.helper` will be inserted during the time of the move. Possible values are a selector (only the first element in the list will be considered), a DOM element, or the string `"parent"` (parent element). The default is `"parent"`.

Table 12-2. Options for managing movable elements

Option	Function
options.cursor	Specifies the `cursor` CSS property when the element moves. It represents the shape of the mouse pointer. The possible values are as follows:
	• `"auto"` (default)
	• `"crosshair"` (a cross)
	• `"default"` (an arrow)
	• `"pointer"` (hand)
	• `"move"` (two crossed arrows)
	• `"e-resize"` (expand to the right)
	• `"ne-resize"` (expand up and right)
	• `"nw-resize"` (expand up and left)
	• `"n-resize"` (expand up)
	• `"se-resize"` (expand down and right)
	• `"sw-resize"` (expand down and left)
	• `"s-resize"` (expand down)
	• `"w-resize"` (expand left)
	• `"text"` (pointer to write text)
	• `"wait"` (hourglass)
	• `"help"` (help pointer)
options.delay	Delay, in milliseconds, after which the first movement of the mouse is taken into account. The displacement may begin after that time. The default is 0.
options.distance	Number of pixels the mouse must be moved before the displacement is taken into account. The default is 1 (i.e., a single pixel is enough to indicate that the user wants to move the item).
options.opacity	Opacity of the element moved when moving. The default is 1.

Specifying and managing swappable elements

The options listed in Table 12-3 allow you to specify which elements can be swapped. By default, all elements that are direct children of the element that calls the `sortable (options)` method are permutable with each other and therefore cannot be swapped with elements of another list. The option in Table 12-4 allows you to change this behavior.

Table 12-3. Options for specifying the swappable elements

Option	Function
`options.items`	Selector representing the swappable elements. By default, this is `"> *"`, which represents all direct children of the element that uses the `sortable (options)` method.
`options.connectWith`	Selector representing the elements in which we can insert our elements. The current swappable elements can be deposited to these other elements, but the reverse is not true (unless the other elements also use `options.connectWith` allowing the deposit to these elements). The default value is `false` (no deposit possible outside the current element).
`options.dropOnEmpty`	If `true`, allows depositing items into an empty list. This option can be used only with `options.connectWith` representing the other possibly empty list.

Table 12-4. Options for managing swappable elements

Option	Function
`options.tolerance`	Indicates how the draggable element should cover the element of deposit for the drop being accepted. The possible values are `"intersect"` (the draggable element covers half of the element of deposit in full) and `"pointer"` (the mouse has entered the element of deposit). The default is `"intersect"`.

Managing empty spaces

When you move an item, it leaves an empty space in the list (the size of the item being moved). jQuery UI places an element of the `ui-sortable-placeholder` class (a *placeholder*) in that location. This element is invisible by default (CSS `visibility` set to hidden), but it is possible to customize it using the options in Table 12-5.

Table 12-5. Options for customizing the placeholder

Option	Function
`options.forcePlaceholderSize`	When set to `true`, takes into account the size of the placeholder when an item is moved. This option is only useful if `options.placeholder` is initialized. The default value is `false`.
`options.placeholder`	CSS class associated with the placeholder, taken into account only if `options.forcePlaceholderSize` is true.

Managing effects at the end of displacement

Once the item is moved, it moves directly to its final position without delay (default operation). We can also produce a visual effect when the element is inserted in the new position (from the location where the mouse was released). This option appears in Table 12-6.

Table 12-6. Options for managing visual effects

Option	Function
options.revert	When set to true, produces a displacement effect on insertion of the element to its new position. It may also indicate of the duration (in milliseconds) for the displacement time. The default value is false (no displacement effect).

Managing displacement constraints

The options listed in Table 12-7 allow you to specify constraints that apply to the item being moved. By default, elements can be moved anywhere on the page, following the movements of the mouse.

Table 12-7. Options for managing displacement constraints

Option	Function
options.grid	Array [x, y] indicating the number of pixels that the element moves horizontally and vertically during displacement of the mouse.
options.axis	Indicates an axis of movement ("x" is horizontal, "y" is vertical). The default value is false (no axis is specified, so displacement is possible in all directions).
options.containment	Indicates an element within which the displacement takes place. The element will be represented by a selector (only the first item in the list will be considered), a DOM element, or the string "parent" (parent element) or "window" (HTML page).
	It may also indicate an array [x1, y1, x2, y2] representing a rectangle formed by the points (x1, y1) and (x2, y2).

Managing window scrolling

You can move an item to locations that are not within the visible portion of the page. For this, we can scroll the page in the browser window. The options for this are listed in Table 12-8.

Table 12-8. Options for managing window scrolling

Option	Function
options.scroll	When set to true (the default), the window will scroll if the item is moved outside the visible part of the display.
options.scrollSensitivity	Indicates how many pixels the mouse must exit the visible area to cause scrolling. The default is 20 pixels. This option is used only with options.scroll set to true.
options.scrollSpeed	Indicates the scrolling speed of the display once the scrolling begins. The default is 20.

Managing events on swappable elements

Events associated with the movable elements can manage the beginning and end of the displacement and the displacement itself. Each of the methods associated with these events has two parameters: event corresponds to the mouse event and ui is a {item, helper, placeholder, sender, offset} object whose properties are described in the following table. The methods are listed in Table 12-9, and the object properties are listed in Table 12-10.

Table 12-9. Options for managing events on swappable elements

Option	Function
options.start	The start (event, ui) method is called when the movement starts (the user clicked on the item and moved the mouse).
options.stop	The stop (event, ui) method is called when the move is complete (the mouse button was released and the moved item is in its final position).
options.beforeStop	The beforeStop (event, ui) method is called before options.stop, while the placeholder is still in the list.
options.sort	The sort (event, ui) method is called when the movement continues after the first move.
options.change	The change (event, ui) method is called when an item has swapped its place with the dragged item. Other permutations can follow.
options.update	The update (event, ui) method is called at the end of the displacement (after options.beforeStop), where the dragged item has swapped its position with another.

Table 12-10. Properties of the ui {item, helper, placeholder, sender, offset} object

Property	Function
item	jQuery class object associated with the item that was clicked (not necessarily the one that moves). See options.helper in Table 12-1).
helper	jQuery class object associated with the element that actually moves (the element that was clicked or the one specified in options.helper).
placeholder	jQuery class object associated with the element that acts as a placeholder (invisible element that reserves the place to drop the item by moving gradually).
sender	jQuery class object associated with the list in which the item originated. This may be null in some methods (e.g., it may be null in options.start and later defined in options.activate).
offset	In all cases, indicates the {top, left} position of the moved element relative to the edges of the page.

Other events are triggered when swapping items between different lists. To switch between different lists, use the connectWith option, which is a selector representing the elements in which we can insert our elements. This will help us determine that an element of an external list was introduced into our list, and also that an element from our list was placed in an external list. Table 12-11 lists the options for managing events that move between lists.

Table 12-11. Options for managing events on the swappable elements of several lists

Option	Function
options.receive	The receive (event, ui) method is called when an external element is introduced in the list (it was added to our list).
options.remove	The remove (event, ui) method is called when the item is placed in an external list (it has been removed from our list).
options.activate	The activate (event, ui) method is called when movement starts for an element (from our list or an external list). This option is especially useful to warning you that an external list has been manipulated.
options.deactivate	The deactivate (event, ui) method is called when an element (from our list or external) has finished moving. This option is especially useful for notification that an external list has been manipulated.

The sortable ("action", params) Method

The sortable ("action", params) method can perform an action on the swappable elements, such as authorizing their displacement. The action is specified as a string in the first argument (e.g., "disable" to inhibit the operation). These actions are listed in Table 12-12.

Table 12-12. The sortable ("action", params) method actions

Action	Function
sortable ("disable")	Disable swapping of items.
sortable ("enable")	Reactivate the permutation of elements.
sortable ("refresh")	Refresh the list of items if necessary.
sortable ("serialize")	Return a serialized string corresponding to the entire list. This can be used in a URL for an Ajax request.
sortable ("toArray")	Return an array of values for items in the list.
sortable ("option", param)	Retrieve the value of the param option indicated. This option corresponds to one of those used with sortable (options).
sortable ("option", param, value)	Change the value of the param option. This option corresponds to one of those used with sortable (options).
sortable ("destroy")	Remove the management of permutation of elements.

Event Management of the Permutation with bind ()

jQuery UI allows us to handle events using the bind () method, detailed in Table 12-13.

Table 12-13. Events created by jQuery UI

Event	Function
sortstart	Same meaning as options.start.
sortstop	Same meaning as options.stop.
sortbeforestop	Same meaning as options.beforeStop.
sort	Same meaning as options.sort.
sortchange	Same meaning as options.change.
sortupdate	Same meaning as options.update.
sortreceive	Same meaning as options.receive.
sortremove	Same meaning as options.remove.
sortactivate	Same meaning as options.activate.
sortdeactivate	Same meaning as options.deactivate.

Examples of Using the Permutation Mechanism

Here are some examples of using the permutation mechanism.

Displaying the Order in Which Events Appear

Items can be moved between two lists or within a single list. First, we'll create a script that allows users to move items within a list, then we'll create a script that allows movement between lists.

When swapping in one list

The goal in this example is to display the order of the events described above, for a single list of items. For this, we display five swappable paragraphs and a <span> element containing the name of events. A line break is added after each stop event:

```
<script src = jquery.js></script>
<script src = jqueryui/js/jquery-ui-1.8.16.custom.min.js></script>

<link rel=stylesheet type=text/css
      href=jqueryui/css/smoothness/jquery-ui-1.8.16.custom.css />

<style type=text/css>
  p.ui-sortable-helper {
    color : red;
  }
</style>

<div id=div1>
  <p> Paragraph 1 </p>
  <p> Paragraph 2 </p>
  <p> Paragraph 3 </p>
```

```
   <p> Paragraph 4 </p>
   <p> Paragraph 5 </p>
</div>

<hr />

<span id=result></span>

<script>

$("#div1").sortable ({
  revert : 1000,
  start : function (event, ui)
  {
    $("span#result").html ($("span#result").html () + "<b>start</b>");
  },
  stop : function (event, ui)
  {
    $("span#result").html ($("span#result").html () + ", stop <br />");
  },
  sort : function (event, ui)
  {
    $("span#result").html ($("span#result").html () + ", sort");
  },
  change : function (event, ui)
  {
    $("span#result").html ($("span#result").html () + ", change");
  },
  beforeStop : function (event, ui)
  {
    $("span#result").html ($("span#result").html () + ", beforeStop");
  },
  update : function (event, ui)
  {
    $("span#result").html ($("span#result").html () + ", update");
  },
  remove : function (event, ui)
  {
    $("span#result").html ($("span#result").html () + ", remove");
  },
  receive : function (event, ui)
  {
    $("span#result").html ($("span#result").html () + ", receive");
  },
  activate : function (event, ui)
  {
    $("span#result").html ($("span#result").html () + ", activate");
  },
  deactivate : function (event, ui)
  {
    $("span#result").html ($("span#result").html () + ", deactivate");
  }
});

</script>
```

After two displacements are made for the first paragraph, you will get a display similar to the one shown in Figure 12-4. The first displacement has not resulted in a permutation, unlike the second (update event). The change events in this second displacement show that two elements have successively switched places with the first paragraph, leading to the final position of the element.

In addition, we see that most of the displayed events are sort events, which correspond to mouse movements.

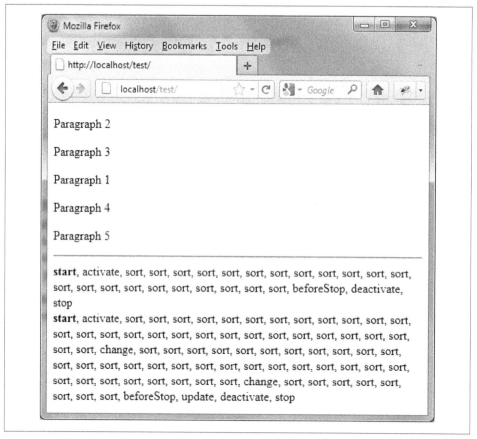

Figure 12-4. Events triggered when switching

If we remove the display of the sort event, the window display is easier to interpret (Figure 12-5):

```
// sort : function (event, ui)
// {
//    $("span#result").html ($("span#result").html () + ", sort");
// },
```

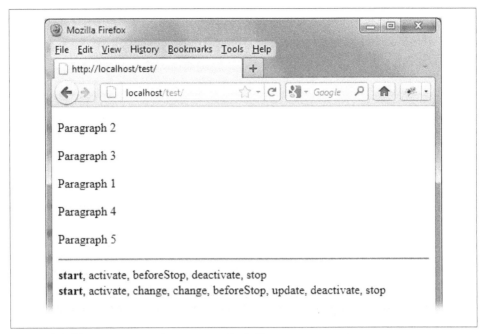

Figure 12-5. The sort events no longer appear in the list

Paragraphs moved in this example are in a single list. Let's see how to allow movement between two lists.

When switching between two lists

We take the same example as above, but this time, we'll use two lists. We allow swapping items between two lists, but also in the same list. For simplicity, we only observe the events from the first list:

```
<script src = jquery.js></script>
<script src = jqueryui/js/jquery-ui-1.8.16.custom.min.js></script>

<link rel=stylesheet type=text/css
      href=jqueryui/css/smoothness/jquery-ui-1.8.16.custom.css />

<style type=text/css>
  p.ui-sortable-helper {
    color : red;
  }
</style>

<div id=div1>
  <p> Paragraph 1 </p>
  <p> Paragraph 2 </p>
  <p> Paragraph 3 </p>
  <p> Paragraph 4 </p>
  <p> Paragraph 5 </p>
```

```
</div>

<hr />

<div id=div2>
  <p> Paragraph 11 </p>
  <p> Paragraph 12 </p>
  <p> Paragraph 13 </p>
  <p> Paragraph 14 </p>
  <p> Paragraph 15 </p>
</div>

<hr />

<span id=result></span>

<script>
$("#div1").sortable ({
  revert : 1000,
  connectWith : "#div2",
  start : function (event, ui)
  {
    $("span#result").html ($("span#result").html () + "<b>start</b>");
  },
  stop : function (event, ui)
  {
    $("span#result").html ($("span#result").html () + ", stop <br />");
  },
// sort : function (event, ui)
// {
//   $("span#result").html ($("span#result").html () + ", sort");
// },
  change : function (event, ui)
  {
    $("span#result").html ($("span#result").html () + ", change");
  },
  beforeStop : function (event, ui)
  {
    $("span#result").html ($("span#result").html () + ", beforeStop");
  },
  update : function (event, ui)
  {
    $("span#result").html ($("span#result").html () + ", update");
  },
  remove : function (event, ui)
  {
    $("span#result").html ($("span#result").html () + ", remove");
  },
  receive : function (event, ui)
  {
    $("span#result").html ($("span#result").html () + ", receive");
  },
  activate : function (event, ui)
  {
```

```
      $("span#result").html ($("span#result").html () + ", activate");
    },
    deactivate : function (event, ui)
    {
      $("span#result").html ($("span#result").html () + ", deactivate");
    }
  });

  $("#div2").sortable ({
    revert : 1000,
    connectWith : "#div1"
  });

</script>
```

The two lists are connected to each other by means of the `connectWith` option. We do not display `sort` events because there are too many!

Figure 12-6 shows the sequence of events shown when we move the first paragraph in the second list. The `change` events were held in the permutations in both the first and second lists. Notice the `remove` event after `update`, showing that the item was removed from that list. If the second list also observed the events, it would have received the `receive` event.

In Figure 12-7, we are moving in the opposite direction. This time, we take the last element of the second list and move it to the beginning of the first list.

The `start` and `stop` events are not received by the first list, but it receives `activate` and `deactivate`. In addition, a single `change` event is received, followed by `receive` and `update`.

Dropping any Element in the List

In this section, we'll work with examples that allow you to create and manage the ability to drop elements in a list.

Inserting images into a list of titles

So far, we have studied only the case where items were swapped between lists. Let's look at what happens if you want to insert an item that is not from another list.

Here, we'll display the titles of some books in a list. This list will contain swappable elements. Then, in another part of the page, we'll display the covers of these books (see Figure 12-8). The goal is to move the covers into the list containing the titles of the books.

You have to move each image to a book title. Figure 12-9 shows two of the covers matched with their titles.

```
<script src = jquery.js></script>
<script src = jqueryui/js/jquery-ui-1.8.16.custom.min.js></script>
```

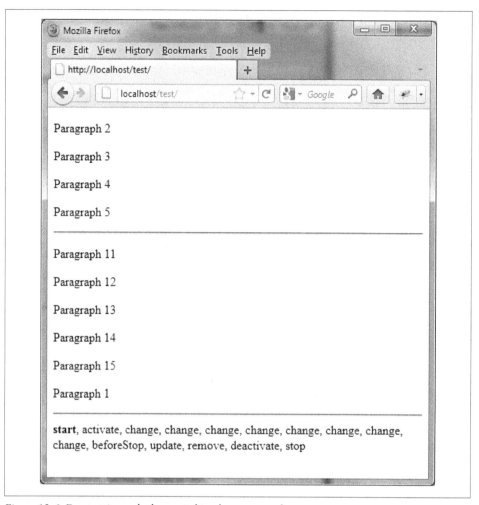

Figure 12-6. Events triggered when switching between two lists

```
<link rel=stylesheet type=text/css
      href=jqueryui/css/smoothness/jquery-ui-1.8.16.custom.css />

<style type=text/css>
  h4 {
    font-family : arial;
    font-size : 12px;
  }
  .placeholder {
    height : 80px;
  }
</style>

<div id=titles>
  <h4> Practical CSS & JavaScript </h4>
```

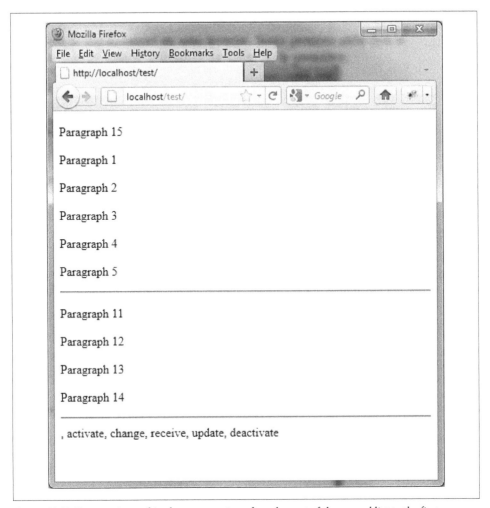

Figure 12-7. Events triggered in the permutation of an element of the second list to the first

```
  <h4> Web development with J2EE </h4>
  <h4> Introduction to HTML & CSS </h4>
  <h4> Practical Ruby on Rails </h4>
</div>

<hr />

<h3> Match each cover with a book title! </h3>
<div id=covers>
  <img src=images/j2ee.jpg height=80 />
  <img src=images/rails.jpg height=80 />
  <img src=images/javascript.jpg height=80 />
  <img src=images/html.jpg height=80 />
</div>
```

Figure 12-8. Associating a book cover with each title in the list

```
<script>

$("div#covers img").draggable ({
  revert : "invalid",
  connectToSortable : "div#titles"
});

$("div#titles").sortable ({
  placeholder : "placeholder",
  forcePlaceholderSize : true,
  sort : function (event, ui)
  {
    ui.placeholder[0].height = ui.helper[0].height;
    ui.placeholder[0].src = ui.helper[0].src;
  },
  receive : function (event, ui)
  {
    ui.item.draggable ("destroy");
  }
});

</script>
```

We specify first that each image can be moved (with the draggable () method). We link each image to the list with the connectToSortable option.

Then the list is identified as switchable (with the sortable () method). We assign a CSS class to options.placeholder so when an image is moved, the vacated location

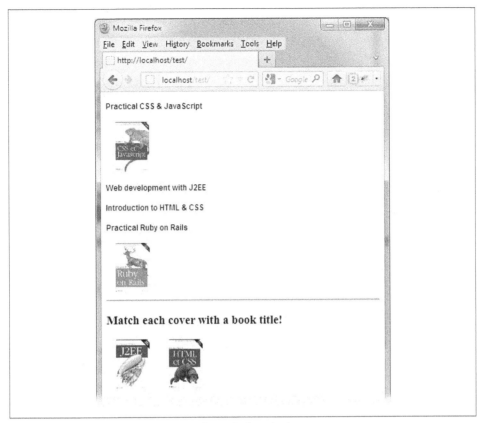

Figure 12-9. The book covers are inserted into the list of titles

retains the height of the image (80 pixels in this case). If you omit this option, you will have an unsightly operation of the script from of a visual point of view.

The sort () method is called for every mouse movement. It initializes the contents of the placeholder with the image of the moved book. If you omit it, the image of the book is not displayed correctly when moving.

The receive () method is used here to inhibit the operation of the draggable () method on the element that was moved into the list. Indeed, this element is now part of the list, so the ability to move it is taken into account by the sortable () method.

Adding a visual treatment

When a book is moved to a title, there is no indication to let users know that the chosen title is correct. Let's add a treatment to see errors in title and cover matching.

We will update the script so that when users match the image of a book to a title, the title appear red only if the match is correct. If the match is incorrect, the title will appear in black (Figure 12-10). We will use the update event, which allows for treatment when an item is placed in the list:

```
<script src = jquery.js></script>
<script src = jqueryui/js/jquery-ui-1.8.16.custom.min.js></script>

<link rel=stylesheet type=text/css
      href=jqueryui/css/smoothness/jquery-ui-1.8.16.custom.css />

<style type=text/css>
  h4 {
    font-family : arial;
    font-size : 12px;
  }
  .placeholder {
    height : 80px;
  }
</style>

<div id=titles>
  <h4 class=javascript> Practical CSS & JavaScript </h4>
  <h4 class=j2ee> Web development with J2EE </h4>
  <h4 class=html> Introduction to HTML & CSS </h4>
  <h4 class=rails> Practical Ruby on Rails </h4>
</div>

<hr />

<h3> Match each cover with a book title! </h3>
<div id=covers>
  <img src=images/j2ee.jpg height=80 class=j2ee />
  <img src=images/rails.jpg height=80 class=rails />
  <img src=images/javascript.jpg height=80 class=javascript />
  <img src=images/html.jpg height=80 class=html />
</div>

<script>

$("div#covers img").draggable ({
  revert : "invalid",
  connectToSortable : "div#titles"
});

$("div#titles").sortable ({
  placeholder : "placeholder",
  forcePlaceholderSize : true,
  sort : function (event, ui)
  {
    ui.placeholder[0].height = ui.helper[0].height;
    ui.placeholder[0].src = ui.helper[0].src;
  },
  receive : function (event, ui)
  {
```

```
      ui.item.draggable ("destroy");
    },
    update : function (event, ui)
    {
      $("div#titles h4").each (function (index)
      {
        var titleClass = this.className;
        var isSameClass = $(this).next().hasClass (titleClass);
        var isOneImg = $(this).next().next ().length == 0 ||
                    !$(this).next().next ()[0].tagName.match (/img/i);
        if (isSameClass && isOneImg) $(this).css ({ "color" : "red" });
        else $(this).css ({ "color" : "black" });
      });
    }
});

</script>
```

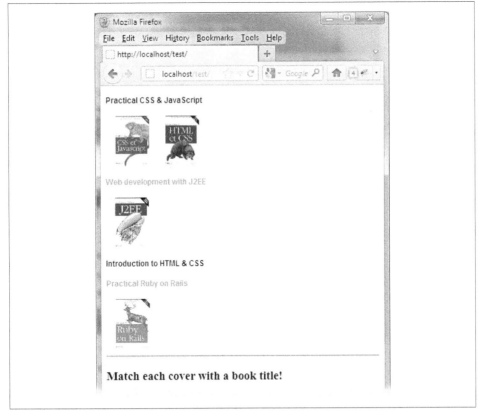

Figure 12-10. Adding a visual treatment to indicate correct matches

We check in the update (event, ui) method whether each title is followed by the image that corresponds to it. For this, we have assigned a CSS class ("html", "javascript", etc.) to each title that is the same for the corresponding image. It is the role of the isSameClass variable to check whether the class of the <h4> element corresponding to the title is the same as the element that follows.

An additional check verifies that not more than one image is associated with a title. Indeed, two images can be moved onto a title. The verification must indicate an error if this occurs (the title appears black, not red).

Resizing

To provide a full range of possibilities for manipulating objects on the page, jQuery UI allows us to resize each element of the page.

Basic Principles of Resizing

Suppose we want to write the HTML code to resize the text display on the screen, as shown in Figure 13-1.

Figure 13-1. Resized text

Here, we have a <p> element containing text (with a border), which can be resized using the mouse (by dragging the right side or the bottom, or by using the resize icon in the bottom right corner).

To allow resizing, we create a <p> element for the item we want to resize. All items displayed are resizable. In addition, we must state the original height or width of the element (required by Internet Explorer, except when one of them is already known, in the case of an image, for example).

And let's not forget, of course, to indicate that the `<p>` element is managed by the jQuery UI `resizable ()` method so that the resize icon appears at the bottom right corner of the item:

```
<script src = jquery.js></script>
<script src = jqueryui/js/jquery-ui-1.8.16.custom.min.js></script>

<link rel=stylesheet type=text/css
      href=jqueryui/css/smoothness/jquery-ui-1.8.16.custom.css />

<p style="border:solid 1px;width:150px">
   A paragraph containing text that resizes!
</p>

<script>

$("p").resizable ();

</script>
```

Formatting Content

The `resizable ()` method displays an icon in the bottom right of the item to resize. In addition, it adds new CSS classes to resizable HTML elements.

In Figure 13-2, for example, the jQuery UI changes the HTML following the `resizable ()` instruction (this code was recovered using the Firebug extension in Firefox).

The `<p>` element was assigned the `ui-resizable` CSS class, while three new `<div>` elements became part of it, as follows (they all have the `ui-resizable-handle` CSS class):

- The right side of the element uses the `ui-resizable-e` CSS class (e indicates East).
- The bottom of the element uses the `ui-resizable-s` CSS class (s indicates South).
- The icon at the bottom right corner of the resizable element uses the `ui-resizable-se` CSS class (se indicates Southeast).

You can use CSS classes of elements to customize the display. For example, if we change the `ui-resizable-e` and `ui-resizable-s` CSS classes, we can prevent scaling on the sides and force the user to resize using only the icon in the lower right corner. To customize the display, simply specify a different value for `width` and `height` properties of these elements (`width` changes the width of the `ui-resizable-e` element, while `height` changes the height of the `ui-resizable-s` element).

Modify these elements in the HTML by adding a `<style>` tag:

```
<script src = jquery.js></script>
<script src = jqueryui/js/jquery-ui-1.8.16.custom.min.js></script>

<link rel=stylesheet type=text/css
      href=jqueryui/css/smoothness/jquery-ui-1.8.16.custom.css />
```

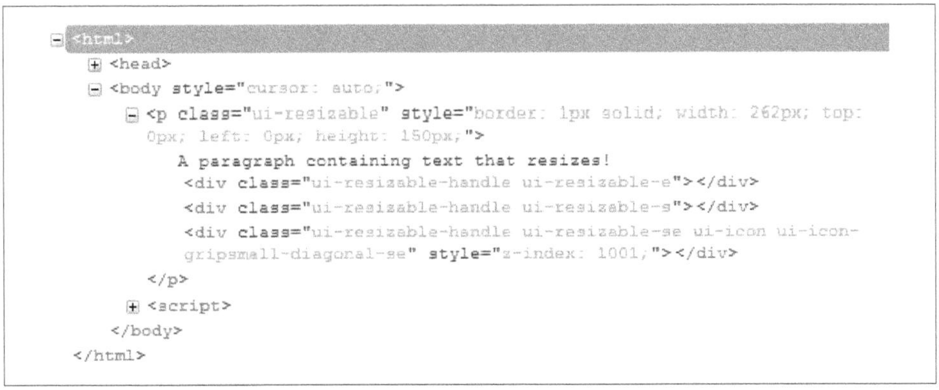

```
<html>
  <head>
  <body style="cursor: auto;">
    <p class="ui-resizable" style="border: 1px solid; width: 262px; top:
      0px; left: 0px; height: 150px;">
        A paragraph containing text that resizes!
        <div class="ui-resizable-handle ui-resizable-e"></div>
        <div class="ui-resizable-handle ui-resizable-s"></div>
        <div class="ui-resizable-handle ui-resizable-se ui-icon ui-icon-
          gripsmall-diagonal-se" style="z-index: 1001;"></div>
    </p>
    <script>
  </body>
</html>
```

Figure 13-2. HTML generated by the resizable () method

```
<style type=text/css>
  .ui-resizable-e {
    width : 0px;
  }
  .ui-resizable-s {
    height : 0px;
  }
</style>

<p style="border:solid 1px;width:150px">
   A paragraph containing text that resizes!
</p>

<script>

$("p").resizable ();

</script>
```

This makes it impossible to resize the element other than by using the icon. We will see in the next section that options allow you to indicate which sides can be resized.

The resizable () Method

The `resizable ()` method can be used under the following two forms:

- `$(selector, context).resizable (options)`
- `$(selector, context).resizable ("action", params)`

The resizable (options) Method

The `resizable (options)` method declares that an HTML element is resizable. The options parameter is an object that specifies behavior when resizing.

Managing resizable elements

We begin with the options to manage the process of resizing (Table 13-1), to indicate which items to resize (Table 13-2), how to resize (Table 13-3), and specify constraints (Table 13-4).

Table 13-1. Options for managing resizable elements

Option	Function
options.disabled	When set to `true`, disables the resizing mechanism. The mouse no longer resizes elements, until the mechanism is enabled (using the `resizable ("enable")` instruction).
options.autoHide	Hides the magnification icon, except when the mouse is over the item.
options.delay	Delay (in milliseconds) before which the first movement of the mouse is taken into account. The displacement will begin thereafter. The default is 0.
options.distance	Distance (in pixels) the mouse must move for resizing to begin. The default is 1 pixel.
options.grid	Array `[x, y]` indicating the number of pixels that the element expands horizontally and vertically during movement of the mouse.

Table 13-2. Options for indicating which elements to resize

Option	Function
options.alsoResize	Selector, jQuery class object, or DOM element representing elements that also resize when resizing the original object. The corresponding elements can be anywhere on the page. The default value is `false` (no other element resizes).
options.cancel	Selector indicating non-resizable elements.

Table 13-3. Options for indicating how to resize

Option	Function
options.aspectRatio	Indicates whether to keep the height and width ratio for the item.
	When set to `true`, the item retains the original ratio of height to width. Otherwise, it indicates a value corresponding to the ratio of the width to the height. For example, 0.5 (one half) indicates that the item must constantly keep a proportion of 1 in width and 2 in height, so that it is always twice as high as it is wide.
	The default value is `false` (no proportion kept).
options.handles	Character string indicating which sides or angles of the element can be resized. The possible values are: n, e, s, and w for the four sides, and ne, se, nw, and sw for the four corners. The letters n, s, e, and w represent the four cardinal points (North, South, East, and West).
	The default is `"e, s, se"`, making it possible to resize the right and bottom, as well as the bottom right corner.

Table 13-4. Options for specifying resizing constraints

Option	Function
`options.containement`	Indicates an element within which the resizing will occur. The item will be represented by a selector (only the first item in the list will be taken into account) or a DOM element, or the string `"parent"` (parent element). The default value is `false` (no constraints).
`options.maxHeight`	Maximum height of the element when resizing. The default is `null` (no constraints).
`options.maxWidth`	Maximum width of the element when resizing. The default is `null` (no constraints).
`options.minHeight`	Minimum height of the element when resizing. The default is `null` (no constraints).
`options.minWidth`	Minimum width of the element when resizing. The default is `null` (no constraints).

Managing resizing effects

The options listed in Table 13-5 allow you to manage visual effects during resizing, either by producing an effect or duplicating the resized element.

Table 13-5. Options for managing resizing effects

Option	Function
`options.animate`	When set to `true`, enables a visual effect during resizing when the mouse button is released. The default value is `false` (no effect).
`options.animateDuration`	Duration (in milliseconds) of the resizing effect. Only used if `options.animate` is `true`.
`options.ghost`	When set to `true`, does not show resizing of the element itself during the resizing operation, but of a less visible ghost element (with a lower opacity). This ghost item will be deleted when the mouse is released.
	The default value is `false` (the element itself is resized).
`options.helper`	CSS class to style the element to be resized. In this case, a new `<div>` element is created, which is the one that is scaled (`ui-resizable-helper` class), then disappears when the mouse button is released.
	The default value is `false` (no new `<div>` element is created).

Managing events on resized elements

Events associated with resizable elements are used to manage the beginning and end of the resizing as well as the resizing in progress. Each of the methods associated with these events (listed in Table 13-6) has two parameters: `event` corresponds to the mouse event, and `ui` is a {`helper, originalPosition, originalSize, position, size`} object whose properties are described in the Table 13-7.

Table 13-6. Options for managing events

Option	Function
options.start	The start (event, ui) method is called when the mouse starts resizing.
options.stop	The stop (event, ui) method is called when the mouse is released. This is the end of the resizing.
options.resize	The resize (event, ui) method is called for every mouse movement during resizing.

Table 13-7. Properties of the ui {helper, originalPosition, originalSize, position, size} object

Property	Function
helper	jQuery class object associated with the element that actually resizes (the element that is clicked, or one created by jQuery UI if you specify a value in options.helper).
originalPosition	A {top, left} object representing the original position of the element.
originalSize	A {width, height} object representing the original dimensions of the element.
position	A {top, left} object representing the current position of the element.
size	A {width, height} object representing the current dimensions of the element.

The resizable ("action", params) Method

The resizable ("action", params) method can perform an action on the resizable elements, such as allowing or preventing resizing. The action is specified as a string in the first argument (e.g., "disable" to inhibit the operation). These actions are listed in Table 13-8.

Table 13-8. The resizable (action", params) method actions

Action	Function
resizable ("disable")	Disable the resizing operation.
resizable ("enable")	Reactivate the resizing operation.
resizable ("option", param)	Retrieve the value of the specified param option. This option corresponds to one of those used with resizable (options).
resizable ("option", param, value)	Change the value of the param option. This option corresponds to one of those used with resizable (options).
resizable ("destroy")	Remove the management of resizing.

Handling Events when Resizing with bind ()

In addition to event methods in the options of the resizable (options) method, jQuery UI allows us to manage these events using the bind () method (listed in Table 13-9).

Table 13-9. Events created by jQuery UI

Event	Function
resizestart	Same meaning as options.start.
resizestop	Same meaning as options.stop.
resize	Same meaning as options.resize.

Examples of Using the Resizing Mechanism

Now that you understand how to use the resizing mechanism, let's look at some resizing examples.

Displaying Dimensions of the Element When Resizing

We can use the resize event to determine the effect of every mouse movement during a resizing operation (see Figure 13-3):

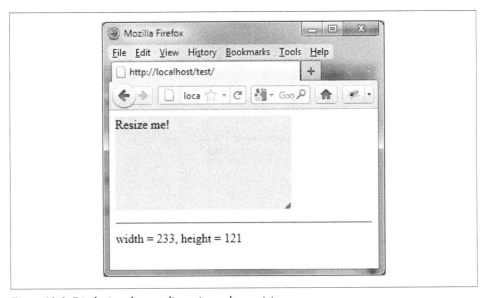

Figure 13-3. Displaying element dimensions when resizing

```
<script src = jquery.js></script>
<script src = jqueryui/js/jquery-ui-1.8.16.custom.min.js></script>

<link rel=stylesheet type=text/css
        href=jqueryui/css/smoothness/jquery-ui-1.8.16.custom.css />

<p style="background-color:gainsboro;width:150px;">
        Resize me!
</p>
```

```
<hr />

<span id=result></span>

<script>

$("p").resizable ({
  resize : function (event, ui)
  {
    $("#result").text ("width = " + ui.size.width +
                      ", height = " + ui.size.height);
  }
});

</script>
```

Displaying the Position of the Element When Resizing

The position of the element is normally fixed on the page. However, this position may change if the element is scaled by its top or left sides. This implies that its top and left coordinates are then modified, therefore, its position on the page changes. Use the following to display position coordinates during resizing:

```
<script src = jquery.js></script>
<script src = jqueryui/js/jquery-ui-1.8.16.custom.min.js></script>

<link rel=stylesheet type=text/css
      href=jqueryui/css/smoothness/jquery-ui-1.8.16.custom.css />

<p style="background-color:gainsboro; width:150px;
        position:absolute;top:100px;left:100px">
    Resize me!
</p>

<span id=result></span>

<hr />

<script>

$("p").resizable ({
  handles : "n, e, s, w, ne, se, nw, sw",
  resize : function (event, ui)
  {
    $("#result").text ("top = " + ui.position.top +
                      ", left = " + ui.position.left +
                      ", width = " + ui.size.width +
                      ", height = " + ui.size.height);
  }
});

</script>
```

By default, the element is positioned at 100, 100. As we enlarge it by the top and left sides (in addition to the bottom and right), its position will change (Figure 13-4).

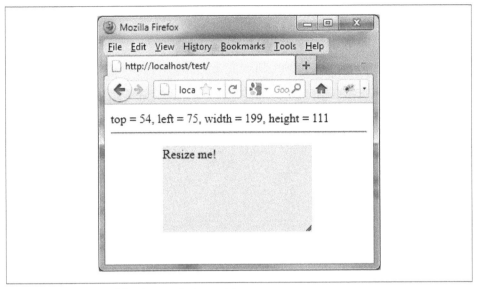

Figure 13-4. Position of the element during resizing

Performing an Animation While Resizing

To produce an animation while resizing, set `options.animate` to true:

```
<script src = jquery.js></script>
<script src = jqueryui/js/jquery-ui-1.8.16.custom.min.js></script>

<link rel=stylesheet type=text/css
      href=jqueryui/css/smoothness/jquery-ui-1.8.16.custom.css />

<p style="background-color:gainsboro; width:150px;">
    Resize me!
</p>

<script>

$("p").resizable ({
  animate : true
});

</script>
```

The element is not immediately resized. The animation occurs only when the mouse button is released. To view the element in the process of resizing, you can also use the `helper` option. It indicates a CSS class that will have the new `<div>` element that will be resized and will be removed when the mouse button is released:

```
<script src = jquery.js></script>
<script src = jqueryui/js/jquery-ui-1.8.16.custom.min.js></script>

<link rel=stylesheet type=text/css
      href=jqueryui/css/smoothness/jquery-ui-1.8.16.custom.css />

<style type=text/css>
  .helper {
    border : dotted 1px red;
  }
</style>

<p style="background-color:gainsboro; width:150px;">
    Resize me!
</p>

<script>

$("p").resizable ({
  animate : true,
  helper : "helper"
});

</script>
```

The red dotted line (shown in Figure 13-5) is the options.helper class element created by jQuery UI. It will disappear when the mouse button is released.

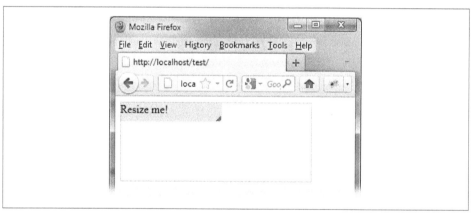

Figure 13-5. Aspect of the element being resized

At the end of resizing operation, the red line disappears and the item appears in its new size (see Figure 13-6).

Figure 13-6. Resized element

Creating a Resizable Text Box

The resizable text box can be on one line or several lines. Here, we'll create examples that implement these two possibilities.

Input on a single line

In a form, rather than having input fields of fixed size, why not allow users to resize themselves if they wish? An example is shown in Figures 13-7 and 13-8. The principle is (almost) the same as for any other element.

The input field must be inserted into another element that will be the one scaled (here, a `<div>` element):

```
<script src = jquery.js></script>
<script src = jqueryui/js/jquery-ui-1.8.16.custom.min.js></script>

<link rel=stylesheet type=text/css
      href=jqueryui/css/smoothness/jquery-ui-1.8.16.custom.css />

<p> Resize the input field!</p>

<div style="width:150px;height:20px">
  <input style="background-color:gainsboro; width:100%;"
         value="Resize me!" />
</div>

<script>

$("div").resizable ({
  handles : "e"
});

</script>
```

We indicate the width and height of the <div> element. Only the height property is mandatory here (if this property is not present, resizing is not enabled in Internet Explorer). The width property set to 150px prevents the input field from spreading over the entire width of the page.

The <input> element has a width property of 100%. This keeps the input field at the same width as the parent element (the <div> element that is resized).

We use the handles option value "e" only, so that expansion can take place only on the right side, otherwise the item could also be expanded in height.

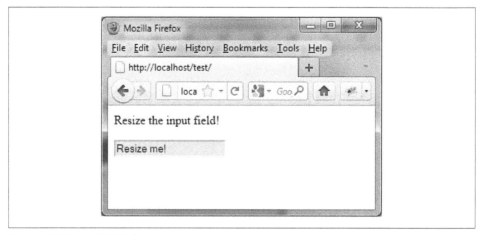

Figure 13-7. Input field before resizing

Figure 13-8. Input field after resizing

Multi-line input

Rather than resizing a single input field for a single line, let's enable resizing of a multi-line input field (a `<textarea>`). Figure 13-9 shows an example.

The principle is the same as before. We insert the `<textarea>` into a `<div>`, which will be the resized element:

```
<script src = jquery.js></script>
<script src = jqueryui/js/jquery-ui-1.8.16.custom.min.js></script>

<link rel=stylesheet type=text/css
      href=jqueryui/css/smoothness/jquery-ui-1.8.16.custom.css />

<p> Resize the multiline input field!</p>

<div style="width:150px;height:40px">
  <textarea style="background-color:gainsboro;
                   width:99%;height:99%">Resize me!
  </textarea>
</div>

<script>

$("div").resizable ();

</script>
```

We indicate a `height` and `width` of 99% rather than 100% so that the resize icon in the lower right is not superimposed on the scroll bars.

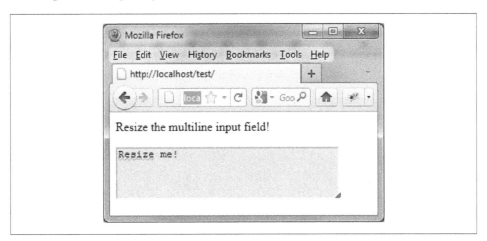

Figure 13-9. Resizing a multi-line input field

Visual Effects in jQuery UI

jQuery supports the use of basic visual effects, including management of the opacity and height of the elements, as well as the management of new effects using the `animate` () method.

jQuery UI also provides the following:

- New visual effects
- Improvement of the `animate` () method
- The ability to use CSS classes to produce effects

New Visual Effects

In addition to the slideUp, slideDown, slideToggle, fadeIn, fadeOut, fadeTo, show, hide, and toggle effects available in standard jQuery, jQuery UI offers a range of new visual effects. All these effects can be used by calling the new `effect` (`effectName`, `options`, `duration`, `callback`) method, which works on jQuery class objects returned by `jQuery` ().

The effect (effectName, options, duration, callback) Method

The `effect` (`effectName`, `options`, `duration`, `callback`) method is used in the following form:

```
$(selector, context).effect (effectName, options, duration, callback)
```

This method allows us to produce the basic visual effects of jQuery UI. The parameters of the method are listed in Table 14-1 (only the first parameter is mandatory).

Table 14-1. The effect () method parameters

Parameter	Function
effectName	String corresponding to the effect name to use ("blind", "bounce", etc.).
optionscallback () method called for each element when the effect is complete for this element. The this value in the function represents the DOM element for which the effect is complete.callback () method called for each element when the effect is complete for this element. The this value in the function represents the DOM element for which the effect is complete.	Optional object to specify the behavior of the effect (e.g., "hide" or "show" in options.mode).
callback () method called for each element when the effect is complete for this element. The this value in the function represents the DOM element for which the effect is complete.callback () method called for each element when the effect is complete for this element. The this value in the function represents the DOM element for which the effect is complete.	
duration	Duration of the effect in milliseconds. Values "slow" and "fast" correspond to periods of 600 and 200 ms. The default duration is 400 ms.
callback	Callback function called for each item in the list (items corresponding to the selector), when the effect is complete for that element. This is an optional parameter.

The blind Effect

The blind effect can hide or display an item, making it disappear or appear in the indicated direction. Options for this effect are listed in Table 14-2.

Table 14-2. Options for managing the blind effect

Option	Function
options.mode	Displays ("show") or hides ("hide") the element. The default value is "hide".
options.direction	The direction ("horizontal" or "vertical") that the element moves to or from when disappearing or appearing. The default value is "vertical".

In the following example, the first image disappears horizontally, while the second appears vertically. Figure 14-1 shows the effect in progress, and Figure 14-2 shows the end result:

```
<script src = jquery.js></script>
<script src = jqueryui/js/jquery-ui-1.8.16.custom.min.js></script>

<link rel=stylesheet type=text/css
      href=jqueryui/css/smoothness/jquery-ui-1.8.16.custom.css />
```

```
<img id=img1 src=images/rails.jpg height=100 /><br />
<img id=img2 src=images/html.jpg height=100 />

<script>

$("#img1").effect ("blind", { mode : "hide", direction : "horizontal" }, 10000);
$("#img2").effect ("blind", { mode : "show", direction : "vertical" }, 10000);

</script>
```

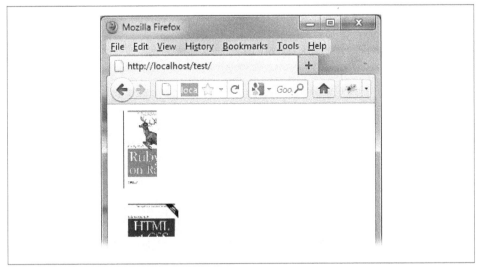

Figure 14-1. The blind effect in progress: the first image disappears horizontally and the second appears vertically

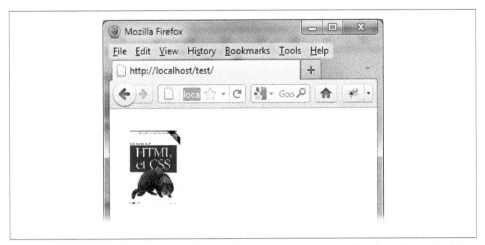

Figure 14-2. The blind effect at completion: the second image has replaced the first, which has completely disappeared

The bounce Effect

The bounce effect makes the element appear to bounce vertically or horizontally as it appears or disappears. Options for this effect are listed in Table 14-3.

Table 14-3. Options for managing the bounce effect

Option	Function
options.mode	Displays ("show") or hides ("hide") the element. The default value is "effect", which means that only the rebound effect is made, without the appearance or disappearance of the element.
options.direction	Direction of the rebound: "up" (the default), "down", "left", or "right".
options.distance	Distance (in pixels) covered during each bounce. The default is 20 pixels.
options.times	Number of bounces to perform. The default is 5.

The shake Effect

The shake effect makes elements appear to shake vertically or horizontally as they appear or disappear. Options for this effect are listed in Table 14-4.

Table 14-4. Options for managing the shake effect

Option	Function
options.direction	Direction of oscillations: "up", "down", "left" (default) or "right".
options.distance	Distance (in pixels) covered during each oscillation. The default is 20 pixels.
options.times	Number of oscillations during the effect. The default is 3.

The clip Effect

The clip effect shows or hides the element by scrolling horizontally or vertically. Options for this effect are listed in Table 14-5.

Table 14-5. Options for managing the clip effect

Option	Function
options.mode	Displays ("show") or hides ("hide") the element. The default value is "hide".
options.direction	Horizontal direction ("horizontal") or vertical direction ("vertical") of the element's appearance or disappearance. The default value is "vertical".

In the following example, only the second book is visible, while the first is not (Figure 14-3). The effect is to remove the second book, while the first appears (Figure 14-4). At the end of the effect, the first book is the only one displayed (Figure 14-5):

```
<script src = jquery.js></script>
<script src = jqueryui/js/jquery-ui-1.8.16.custom.min.js></script>

<link rel=stylesheet type=text/css
      href=jqueryui/css/smoothness/jquery-ui-1.8.16.custom.css />

<img id=img1 src=images/rails.jpg height=100 /><br />
<img id=img2 src=images/html.jpg height=100 />

<script>

$("#img1").effect ("clip", { mode : "show" }, 10000);
$("#img2").effect ("clip", { mode : "hide" }, 10000);

</script>
```

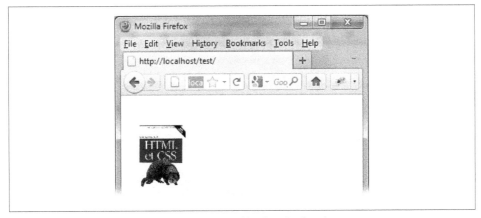

Figure 14-3. Before the clip effect: only the second book is displayed

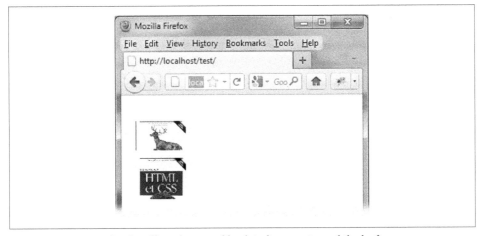

Figure 14-4. During the clip effect: the second book is disappearing, while the first appears

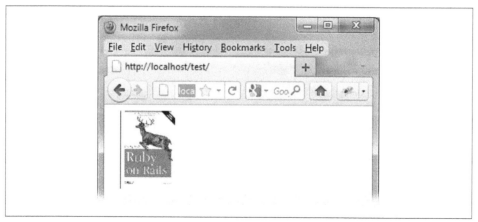

Figure 14-5. End of effect: only the first book is displayed

The drop Effect

The drop effect shows or hides the item by dragging and lowering its opacity. Options for this effect are listed in Table 14-6.

Table 14-6. Options for managing the drop effect

Option	Function
options.mode	Displays ("show") or hides ("hide") the element. The default value is "hide".
options.direction	Direction indicates the direction of movement "up", "down", "left" (default), or "right".
options.distance	Distance (in pixels) covered by the element.

Here is an example of using the drop effect. In this example, the first book appears and the second book disappears. The result is shown in Figure 14-6:

```
<script src = jquery.js></script>
<script src = jqueryui/js/jquery-ui-1.8.16.custom.min.js></script>

<link rel=stylesheet type=text/css
      href=jqueryui/css/smoothness/jquery-ui-1.8.16.custom.css />

<img id=img1 src=images/rails.jpg height=100 /><br />
<img id=img2 src=images/html.jpg height=100 />

<script>

$("#img1").effect ("drop", { mode : "show" }, 1000);
$("#img2").effect ("drop", { mode : "hide" }, 1000);

</script>
```

Figure 14-6. The drop effect

The explode Effect

The explode effect makes the element appear or disappear in a burst, as if it is exploding (see Figure 14-7). The options for this effect are listed in Table 14-7.

Table 14-7. Options for managing the explode effect

Option	Function
options.mode	Specifies whether you want to display ("show") or hide ("hide") the element. The default value is "hide".
options.pieces	The number of pieces of the burst element. The default is 9.

```
<script src = jquery.js></script>
<script src = jqueryui/js/jquery-ui-1.8.16.custom.min.js></script>

<link rel=stylesheet type=text/css
      href=jqueryui/css/smoothness/jquery-ui-1.8.16.custom.css />

<img id=img1 src=images/rails.jpg height=100 /><br />
<img id=img2 src=images/html.jpg height=100 />

<script>
```

```
$("#img1").effect ("explode", { mode : "show" }, 1000);
$("#img2").effect ("explode", { mode : "hide" }, 1000);

</script>
```

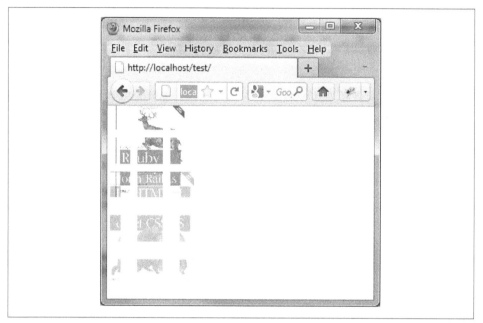

Figure 14-7. The explode effect

The fold Effect

The fold effect can show or hide the item by progressing horizontally, then vertically (or vice versa—the order is specified by `options.horizFirst`). The options for this effect are listed in Table 14-8

Table 14-8. Options for managing the fold effect

Option	Function
options.mode	Displays ("show") or hides ("hide") the element. The default value is "hide".
options.horizFirst	When set to true, to the effect starts with horizontal progression, followed by vertical (the reverse occurs when this option is set to false). The default value is false.
options.size	Indicates the number of pixels of the first progression (horizontal or vertical). The default value is 15 pixels.

```
<script src = jquery.js></script>
<script src = jqueryui/js/jquery-ui-1.8.16.custom.min.js></script>

<link rel=stylesheet type=text/css
      href=jqueryui/css/smoothness/jquery-ui-1.8.16.custom.css />

<img id=img1 src=images/rails.jpg height=100 /><br />
<img id=img2 src=images/html.jpg height=100 />

<script>

$("#img1").effect ("fold", { mode : "show", horizFirst : true,
                             size : 75 }, 1000);
$("#img2").effect ("fold", { mode : "hide", size : 75 }, 1000);

</script>
```

The highlight Effect

The highlight effect can show or hide an element by changing its background color, as shown in Figures 14-8 and 14-9. The options for this effect are listed in Table 14-9.

Table 14-9. Options for managing the highlight effect

Option	Function
options.mode	Displays ("show") or hides ("hide") the element. The default value is "show".
options.color	Initial background color of the element, which will progress to get to the original background color.

```
<script src = jquery.js></script>
<script src = jqueryui/js/jquery-ui-1.8.16.custom.min.js></script>

<link rel=stylesheet type=text/css
      href=jqueryui/css/smoothness/jquery-ui-1.8.16.custom.css />

<p id=p1> Paragraph 1 </p>
<p id=p2> Paragraph 2 </p>

<script>

$("#p1").effect ("highlight", { mode : "hide", color : "black" }, 10000);
$("#p2").effect ("highlight", { mode : "show", color : "black" }, 10000);

</script>
```

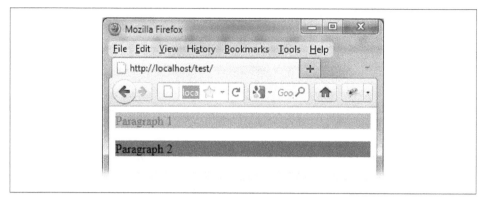

Figure 14-8. The highlight effect: the first paragraph disappears, while the second appears

In Figure 14-9, the second paragraph is completely visible and has a white background.

Figure 14-9. End of the highlight effect: paragraph 1 has disappeared to make room for paragraph 2

The puff Effect

The puff effect shows or hides the element by enlarging or shrinking it and changing its opacity. The options for this effect are listed in Table 14-10.

Table 14-10. Options for managing the puff effect

Option	Function
options.mode	Displays ("show") or hides ("hide") the element. The default value is "hide".
options.percent	Percentage magnification of the element (if options.mode is "hide"), or narrowing (finally arriving at its original size, if options.mode is "show"). The default is 150%.

In this example, the first book appears by returning to its normal size, while the second gets bigger as it disappears. The result is shown in Figure 14-10:

```
<script src = jquery.js></script>
<script src = jqueryui/js/jquery-ui-1.8.16.custom.min.js></script>

<link rel=stylesheet type=text/css
     href=jqueryui/css/smoothness/jquery-ui-1.8.16.custom.css />

<img id=img1 src=images/rails.jpg height=100 /><br />
<img id=img2 src=images/html.jpg height=100 />

<script>

$("#img1").effect ("puff", { mode : "show" }, 1000);
$("#img2").effect ("puff", { mode : "hide" }, 1000);

</script>
```

Figure 14-10. The puff effect

The pulsate Effect

The pulsate effect causes the element to flash. The number of flashes (default 5) is specified using the options.times option. Each blink corresponds to the duration of the effect:

```
<script src = jquery.js></script>
<script src = jqueryui/js/jquery-ui-1.8.16.custom.min.js></script>

<link rel=stylesheet type=text/css
     href=jqueryui/css/smoothness/jquery-ui-1.8.16.custom.css />
```

```
<img id=img1 src=images/rails.jpg height=100 /><br />
<img id=img2 src=images/html.jpg height=100 />

<script>

$("#img1").effect ("pulsate", { times : 2 }, 1000);
$("#img2").effect ("pulsate", { times : 5 }, 1000);

</script>
```

The scale Effect

The scale effect enlarges or shrinks the element. It can also make the element appear or disappear, depending on the option indicated in options.mode. The options for this effect are listed in Table 14-11.

Table 14-11. Options for managing the scale effect

Option	Function
options.mode	Displays ("show") or hides ("hide") the element. The default value is "effect", (only the scaling effect is performed, without the appearance or disappearance of the element).
options.direction	Indicates the direction of resizing: "horizontal", "vertical", or "both". The default is "both".
options.from	A {width, height} object indicating the original dimensions of the element. By default, the current size of the element is taken as the original dimensions.
options.percent	Percentage to magnify (if greater than 100) or shrink (if less than 100). The default is 0 if options.mode is "hide", or 100 if options.mode is "show".
options.fade	When set to true, changes the opacity of the element when resizing. The default value is false.

```
<script src = jquery.js></script>
<script src = jqueryui/js/jquery-ui-1.8.16.custom.min.js></script>

<link rel=stylesheet type=text/css
      href=jqueryui/css/smoothness/jquery-ui-1.8.16.custom.css />

<img id=img1 src=images/rails.jpg height=100 /><br />
<img id=img2 src=images/html.jpg height=100 />

<script>

$("#img1").effect ("scale", { mode : "show" }, 10000);
$("#img2").effect ("scale", { mode : "hide" }, 10000);

</script>
```

The size Effect

Rather than expanding in the same proportions as height and width as allowed by the scale effect, the size effect applies a new height and width to the element. This is done using options.to with a {width, height} object. If either the width or height property is not indicated in options.to, the element is not expanded in that direction (width or height). Options for this effect are listed in Table 14-12.

Table 14-12. Options for managing the size effect

Option	Function
options.from	A {width, height} object indicating the original dimensions of the element. By default, the current size of the element is taken as the original dimensions.
options.to	A {width, height} object indicating the final dimensions of the element. By default, the current size of the element is taken as the final dimensions.

For example, to expand our image to 300 pixels in width, keeping a height of 100 pixels (see Figure 14-11), we write the following code:

```
<script src = jquery.js></script>
<script src = jqueryui/js/jquery-ui-1.8.16.custom.min.js></script>

<link rel=stylesheet type=text/css
      href=jqueryui/css/smoothness/jquery-ui-1.8.16.custom.css />

<img id=img1 src=images/rails.jpg height=100 /><br />

<script>

$("#img1").effect ("size", { to : { width : 300 } }, 1000);

</script>
```

Figure 14-11. The size effect

The slide Effect

The slide effect shows or hides the item by sliding it across the screen. Options for this effect are listed in Table 14-13.

Table 14-13. Options for managing the slide effect

Option	Function
options.mode	Displays ("show") or hides ("hide") the element. The default value is "hide".
options.direction	Indicates the direction of movement: "up", "down", "left", (default) or "right".
options.distance	Distance (in pixels) covered by the element. The default is the height of the element (if options.direction is "up" or "down") or the width of the element (if options.direction is "left" or "right").

For example, to display the first book while making disappear the second, we write the following code:

```
<script src = jquery.js></script>
<script src = jqueryui/js/jquery-ui-1.8.16.custom.min.js></script>

<link rel=stylesheet type=text/css
      href=jqueryui/css/smoothness/jquery-ui-1.8.16.custom.css />

<img id=img1 src=images/rails.jpg height=100 /><br />
<img id=img2 src=images/html.jpg height=100 />

<script>

$("#img1").effect ("slide", { mode : "show" }, 10000);
$("#img2").effect ("slide", { mode : "hide" }, 10000);

</script>
```

The show (), hide (), and toggle () Methods

The above effects use the mode option to hide ("hide") or display ("show") the element.

Rather than specifying this option in the options parameter, jQuery UI allows us to specify it using the show () or hide () methods. As for the toggle () method, it toggles the show () or hide () methods depending on whether the element is hidden or not.

Use the following to display an item using the indicated effect:

```
$(selector, context).show (effectName, options, duration, callback);
```

Use the following to hide an item using the indicated effect:

```
$(selector, context).hide (effectName, options, duration, callback);
```

Use the following to change between showing and hiding the indicated effect:

```
$(selector, context).toggle (effectName, options, duration, callback);
```

For example, let's use these methods with the slide effect instead of the effect ()
method that we used before. We create a Toggle button, which, when clicked, shows
or hides the element by using the slide effect (see Figure 14-12).

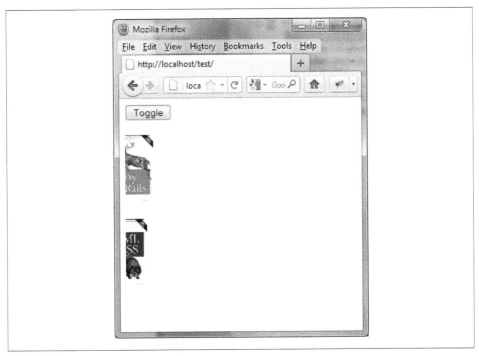

Figure 14-12. Using the toggle () method

```
<script src = jquery.js></script>
<script src = jqueryui/js/jquery-ui-1.8.16.custom.min.js></script>

<link rel=stylesheet type=text/css
      href=jqueryui/css/smoothness/jquery-ui-1.8.16.custom.css />

<button onclick=toggle()>Toggle </button><br /><br />

<img id=img1 src=images/rails.jpg height=100 /><br />
<img id=img2 src=images/html.jpg height=100 style=display:none />

<script>

function toggle ()
{
  $("#img1").toggle ("slide", 10000);
  $("#img2").toggle ("slide", 10000);
}

</script>
```

The animate () method Improved by jQuery UI

The jQuery animate () method, which allows visual effects by changing CSS properties, has a number of limitations on CSS properties associated with the color and easing options (setting progression in the effect). Thanks to jQuery UI, it is possible to implement improved effects.

CSS Properties for Managing Colors

Unlike the jQuery animate () method, jQuery UI allows the use of color CSS properties such as color, background-color, border-color, etc.

In the following example, we want to create an effect to gradually change the background and character colors of two paragraphs: initially in black letters on a white background (Figure 14-13), the elements gradually change into white characters (color: "white") on a black background ("background-color": "black"). Figure 14-14 shows this effect in progress, and the final result is shown in Figure 14-15:

```
<script src = jquery.js></script>
<script src = jqueryui/js/jquery-ui-1.8.16.custom.min.js></script>

<link rel=stylesheet type=text/css
        href=jqueryui/css/smoothness/jquery-ui-1.8.16.custom.css />

<p> Paragraph 1 </p>
<p> Paragraph 2 </p>

<script>

$("p").animate ({
   "background-color" : "black",
   color : "white"
}, 10000);

</script>
```

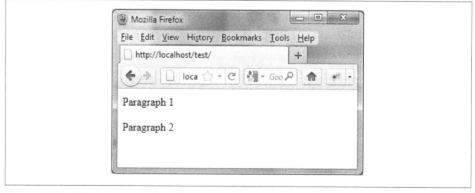

Figure 14-13. The two paragraphs before applying the effect

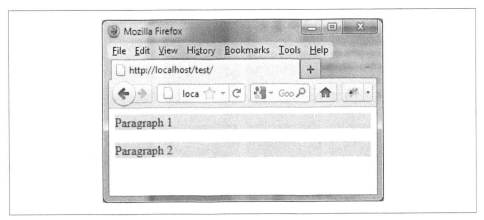

Figure 14-14. Changing colors with the animate () method: intermediate step

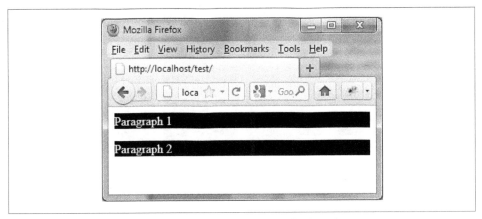

Figure 14-15. Changing colors with the animate () method: final result

New Values for the easing Option

The jQuery animate () method supports the linear and swing values for the easing option. Remember that this option specifies how to progress into the effect: faster at first, faster at the end, and so on.

The new values of the easing option are shown in Figures 14-16 and 14-17 provided on the jQuery UI official site (*http://jqueryui.com/docs/effect/easing*). The curve allows you to view how to progress in the effect.

Producing Effects with CSS Classes

jQuery methods for managing CSS classes have been improved in jQuery UI to manage the visual effects.

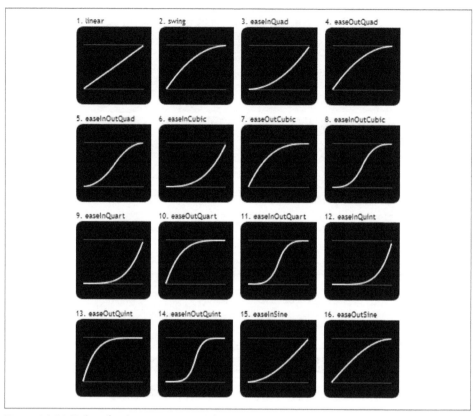

Figure 14-16. Values for the easing option (1)

The addClass (), removeClass (), and toggleClass () Improved Methods

jQuery UI has also improved the addClass (), removeClass (), and toggleClass () methods provided by jQuery. The options for these classes are listed in Table 14-14.

The new form of the addClass () method is:

```
$(selector, context).addClass (className, duration, easing, callback);
```

The new form of the removeClass () method is:

```
$(selector, context).removeClass (className, duration, easing, callback);
```

The new form of the toggleClass () method is:

```
$(selector, context).toggleClass (className, addOrRemove, duration,
                                  easing, callback);
```

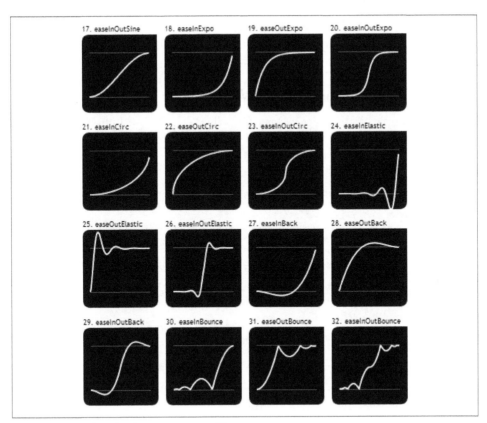

Figure 14-17. Values for the easing option (2)

Table 14-14. The toggleClass () method parameters

Parameter	Function
className	String containing one or more CSS classes (separated by spaces).
duration	Indicates the number of milliseconds of the effect. A value of 0 takes the element directly in the new style, without progressivity.
easing	Indicates the way to progress in the effect.
callback	callback () method called for each element when the effect is complete for this element. This value in the function represents the DOM element for which the effect is complete.
addOrRemove	Optional Boolean indicating whether to add the CSS class (if true) or delete it (if false). If not specified, the CSS is removed if present.

The switchClass () Method

In addition to the improvement of the addClass (), removeClass (), and toggleClass () methods, jQuery UI includes a new switchClass () method to move from one CSS class to another.

The switchClass () method has the following form:

```
$(selector, context). switchClass (classNameRemoved,classNameAdded, duration,
                                    easing, callback);
```

Example of Using the toggleClass () Method

Here is an example of using toggleClass () method. The Toggle button allows you to add or remove a CSS class (here, class1) on each paragraph by producing an effect. Once the new style is applied (after the first click), click the button again to restore the original style (Figures 14-18 and 14-19).

The CSS border-style property is not scalable, and it is not integrated into the CSS class:

```
<script src = jquery.js></script>
<script src = jqueryui/js/jquery-ui-1.8.16.custom.min.js></script>

<link rel=stylesheet type=text/css
      href=jqueryui/css/smoothness/jquery-ui-1.8.16.custom.css />

<style type=text/css>
  .class1 {
    border-width : 10px;
    border-color : red;
    background-color : black;
    color : white;
  }
</style>

<button onclick=toggle()> Toggle </button>

<p style=border-style:solid> Paragraph 1 </p>
<p style=border-style:solid> Paragraph 2 </p>

<script>

function toggle ()
{
  $("p").toggleClass ("class1", 1000);
}

</script>
```

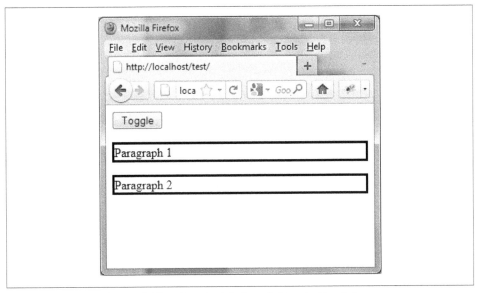

Figure 14-18. Using the toggleClass () method: before clicking the Toggle button

Figure 14-19. Using the toggleClass () method: after clicking the Toggle button

About the Author

Eric Sarrion has written about Rails, HTML and CSS, J2EE, and JavaScript for O'Reilly France. He manages a small training and development company.

Get even more for your money.

Join the O'Reilly Community, and register the O'Reilly books you own. It's free, and you'll get:

- $4.99 ebook upgrade offer
- 40% upgrade offer on O'Reilly print books
- Membership discounts on books and events
- Free lifetime updates to ebooks and videos
- Multiple ebook formats, DRM FREE
- Participation in the O'Reilly community
- Newsletters
- Account management
- 100% Satisfaction Guarantee

Signing up is easy:

1. **Go to: oreilly.com/go/register**
2. **Create an O'Reilly login.**
3. **Provide your address.**
4. **Register your books.**

Note: English-language books only

To order books online:
oreilly.com/store

For questions about products or an order:
orders@oreilly.com

To sign up to get topic-specific email announcements and/or news about upcoming books, conferences, special offers, and new technologies:
elists@oreilly.com

For technical questions about book content:
booktech@oreilly.com

To submit new book proposals to our editors:
proposals@oreilly.com

O'Reilly books are available in multiple DRM-free ebook formats. For more information:
oreilly.com/ebooks

O'REILLY®

Spreading the knowledge of innovators   oreilly.com

Have it your way.

Ingram Content Group UK Ltd.
Milton Keynes UK
UKHW032129150323
418636UK00007B/388